THE LOVE OF ETERNAL WISDOM

by

ST. LOUIS-MARIE
DE MONTFORT

Translated from the French

and Annotated

by

A. Somers, S.M.M.

Revised Edition

ISBN 0-910984-05-0

MONTFORT PUBLICATIONS
26 S. SAXON AVE.
BAYSHORE, N.Y. 11706-8993

Imprimi Potest:

> FRANK A. SETZER, S.M.M.,
> > *Provincial Superior.*

Nihil Obstat:

> MARTIN J. HEALY, S.T.D.,
> > *Censor Librorum.*

Imprimatur:

> ✠ WALTER P. KELLENBERG, D.D.,
> > *Bishop of Rockville Centre.*

May 27, 1960.

1960	1st Printing	10,000
1980	2nd Printing	5,000
1986	3rd Printing	5,000
1992	4th Printing	5,000

CONTENTS

iii

FOREWORD

In this little book, *Love of Eternal Wisdom*, St. Louis-Marie de Montfort gives us a valuable abridgment of his spirituality which can be summed up in the words of St. Paul: "Christ living in us."

Christ lives in all Christians who are in the state of grace. In the great majority, however, the Christian life is only, as it were, in its embryo. Montfort's aim is to develop that embryo until Christ has come to the fullness of His age in us. That is, until we have become perfect Christians. According to Montfort this perfect Christian life is acquired by an ardent desire, continual prayer, universal mortification and a tender and true devotion to the Blessed Virgin Mary.

Among these four means Montfort stresses devotion to Mary as the surest, the easiest and the quickest way to the perfect development of the Christ-life in us.

In the last Chapter of this book he gives us a succinct and clear summary of his treatise, entitled *A Tender and True Devotion to the Blessed Virgin.* Those who find difficulty in understanding his *Treatise on True Devotion to Mary* will be greatly assisted by reading the last Chapter of *Love of Eternal Wisdom.*

It is unfortunate and a loss to the spiritual life of many that Montfort's great devotion to Jesus

Christ, Eternal Wisdom, is not so well known as his devotion to the Blessed Virgin.

This little book written by St. Louis De Montfort places devotion to Mary in its true perspective, and will be of immense value to all lovers of our Lady, especially to those who have consecrated themselves to her as her slaves of love.

Divine Wisdom, Jesus Christ, is the Treasure of all treasures. He was made for us. We are made for Him.

Whoever patiently reads this work and faithfully practices its teachings will find a magnificent reward in the possession of this treasure.

May our Lady the Mother and Seat of Divine Wisdom obtain that grace for all the readers of this little book.

DEDICATORY PRAYER TO ETERNAL WISDOM

1. *O Divine Wisdom! O Lord of heaven and earth! Humbly prostrate before You, I beg pardon for daring to speak of Your greatness, ignorant and guilty as I am. Consider not, I pray You, the darkness of my mind or the uncleanness of my lips, unless it be to dispel them with a glance of Your eyes and a breath of Your mouth. There is in You so much beauty and delight; You have shielded me from so many evils and showered on me so many favors, yet You are so little known and so much slighted! How can You expect me to be silent? Not only justice and gratitude but my own interests compel me to speak of You, albeit falteringly like a child. I can but stammer, it is true, but then I am still only a child anxious to learn how to speak properly through my lisping, until I have attained the fulness of Your age on earth.*

2. *I admit there seems to be neither sense nor order in what I am writing; but my desire to possess You is so ardent that like Solomon I seek You everywhere, wandering and turning in every direction.[1] And if I am trying to make You known to the world, it is because You have promised that all those who explain You and make You known shall have life everlasting.[2] Deign then, O loving Lord, to listen to my feeble stammerings as though they were a masterly discourse. Deign to consider every stroke of my pen as so many efforts on my part to find You; and bestow, from Your high throne above, so much grace and light on what I intend to do and to say about You,*

that all those who read it may be inflamed with a new desire to love and possess You in time and in eternity. Amen.

[1]*"I went about seeking, that I might take her to myself"* (Wisdom VIII, 18).
[2]*"They that explain Thee shall have life everlasting"* (Eccli. XXIV, 31).

Admonitions of Eternal Wisdom

To the mighty and the rulers of this world; taken from the Book of Wisdom, Chapter Six.

1. "WISDOM *is better than strength: and a wise man is better than a strong man.*

"*Hear therefore, ye kings, and understand: learn, ye that are judges of the ends of the earth. Give ear, you that rule the people, and that please yourselves in multitudes of nations.* . . .

Seek After God

2. "*Wisdom is glory, and never fadeth away, and is easily seen by them that love her, and is found by them that seek her. She preventeth them that covet her, so that she first showeth herself unto them. He that awaketh early to seek her shall not labor: for he shall find her sitting at his door. To think therefore upon her is perfect understanding: and he that watcheth for her shall quickly be secure. For she goeth about seeking such as are worthy of her: and she showeth herself to them cheerfully in the ways and meeteth them with all providence.*

3. *For the beginning of her is the most true desire of discipline. And the care of discipline is love: and love is the keeping of the laws: and the keeping of*

*the laws is the firm foundation of incorruption: And
incorruption bringeth near to God. Therefore the desire of wisdom bringeth to the everlasting kingdom.
If then your delight be in thrones and scepters, O
ye kings of the people, love wisdom, that you may
reign for ever. Love the light of wisdom, all ye that
bear rule over peoples.*

Listen To His Instructions

*4. Now what wisdom is, and what was her origin,
I will declare. And I will not hide from you the
mysteries of God, but will seek her out from the
beginning of her birth, and bring the knowledge of
her to light, and will not pass over the truth.
Neither will I go with consuming envy: for such
a man shall not be partaker of wisdom. Now the
multitude of the wise is the welfare of the whole
world: and the wise king is the upholding of the
people. Receive therefore instruction by my words:
and it shall be profitable to you."*

5. In this Chapter, dear reader, I have refrained
from mingling the weakness of my words with the
authority of the Holy Spirit. But let us consider
the following truths:

(1) Of Himself Eternal Wisdom is most meek,
accessible and attractive, whilst being also most resplendent, excellent and sublime. He draws us to
Himself to teach us the way to happiness; He seeks

us; He pleases us by bestowing many gifts upon us; He forestalls us in many different ways; He is even waiting for us, seated at our very door, to give us tokens of His love. Who is there that has a heart and yet would not give it to this gentle conqueror?

6. (2) Great is the misfortune of the mighty and the rich if they do not love Eternal Wisdom. The words He speaks to them are terrifying. They cannot be rendered in our language.

"Horribly and speedily will He appear to you . . . the mighty shall be mightily tormented . . . a greater punishment is ready for the more mighty." [1]

To these words let us add a few which He spoke to them after His Incarnation.

"Woe to you that are rich." [2]

"It is easier for a camel to pass through the eye of a needle than for a rich man to enter into the kingdom of God." [3]

"Go now, ye rich man, weep and howl in your miseries, which shall come upon you." [4]

These last words were so often repeated by Divine Wisdom when He lived on earth that three Evangelists have quoted them without variation, which ought to make the rich weep and wail and lament.

But alas, they have their earthly comforts, they are as it were, bewitched by their pleasures and riches; they do not see the evils which hang over their heads.

7. (3) Solomon assures us that he will give a

faithful and an exact description of wisdom, and that neither envy nor pride, which are contrary to charity, will prevent him from teaching this knowledge which he received from heaven. Nor does he fear being outmatched or equaled by others.

After the example of this great man I shall explain in simple terms what Eternal Wisdom is *before* His Incarnation; *in* His Incarnation, and *after* His Incarnation, and also the *means* to possess and keep Him.

But as I have not the abundance of knowledge and light which Solomon had, I need not fear envy and pride so much as my insufficiency and ignorance. These, I pray you, in your charity, to bear with and to excuse.

---

[1] Wisdom 6:6, 7, 9;   [2] Luke 6:24;   [3] Luke 18:25;
[4] James 5:1.

CHAPTER ONE

To Love and Seek Eternal Wisdom, it is Necessary to Know Him

8. Is it possible for man to love that which he does not know? Can he love ardently that which he knows but imperfectly? Why then is the adorable Jesus, Eternal and Incarnate Wisdom, loved so little? Because He is not known, or known but little. Very few of us, like St. Paul, make a sincere study of the supereminent science of Jesus which is nevertheless the most noble, the most consoling, the most useful and the most necessary of all sciences in heaven and on earth.

9. First: This is the most noble of all sciences because its object, the Uncreated and Incarnate Wisdom, is most noble and most sublime. He contains in Himself all the plenitude of the Divinity and of humanity, all that is great in heaven and on earth, all creatures visible and invisible, spiritual and corporeal. St. John Chrysostom tells us that Our Lord is a summary of all the works of God; an epitome of all God's perfections and of all the perfections of His creatures, in these words: "Jesus Christ, Eternal Wisdom, is all that you can and should wish for. Long for Him, seek Him; He is the most precious pearl you should wish to acquire, even at the cost of selling all that you possess." Furthermore, the Prophet Jeremias warns: "Let not the wise man glory in his wisdom; let not the strong man glory in

his strength, let not the rich man glory in his riches; but let him that glorieth glory in this, that he understandeth and knoweth Me," [1] and not in the fact that he knoweth anything else.

10. Second: Nothing is more consoling than to know Divine Wisdom. Blessed are they who listen to Him; more blessed still they who long for Him and seek after Him. Blessed above all are they who teach His ways, who experience within their hearts the intimate sweetness of Him Who is at once the joy and happiness of the Eternal Father and the glory of the Angels.

If we knew the delight of a soul that knows the beauty of Divine Wisdom and that is nourished at the bosom of the Father; we should exclaim with the Spouse: "Thy breasts are better than wine." [2] Better, too, than all creature delights, especially when He says to those who contemplate Him: "Taste and see"; "and be inebriated" with My eternal delights, "for My conversation hath no bitterness, nor My company any tediousness, but joy and gladness." [3]

11. Third: This knowledge of Eternal Wisdom is not only the most noble and consoling, it is also the most useful and the most necessary, because "Eternal Life is to know God and His Son Jesus Christ." [4] "To know Thee," exclaims the Wise Man, speaking of Wisdom, "is perfect justice, and to know thy justice and thy power is the root of immortality." [5]

If we really wish to obtain life everlasting, let us acquire knowledge of Divine Wisdom; if we wish to reach perfect sanctity on earth, let us know Eternal Wisdom; if we wish to possess the root of immortality in our heart, let us have in our mind knowledge of Eternal Wisdom. TO KNOW JESUS CHRIST, ETERNAL WISDOM, IS TO KNOW ENOUGH; TO KNOW EVERYTHING AND NOT TO KNOW HIM, IS TO KNOW NOTHING.

12. What does it avail an archer to know how to hit the outer parts of the target, if he does not know how to hit the center?

What will it avail us to know all other sciences necessary for salvation, if we do not know the only essential one, the center to which all others must converge, Jesus Christ?

Although St. Paul was a man of varied knowledge and well versed in human sciences, he said: "I judge not myself to know anything among you but Jesus Christ, and Him crucified." [6] Let us say with him, then, "The things that were given to me, the same I have counted loss for Christ. I count all things to be but loss for the excellent knowledge of Jesus Christ, my Lord." [7] I now see and appreciate that this knowledge is so excellent, so delightful, so profitable and so admirable that I take no account of all that pleased me before. All else is void of meaning, absurd and a waste of time. "This I say, that no man may deceive you by loftiness of words. Beware

3

lest any man cheat you by philosophy and vain deceit." [8] I say to you that Jesus Christ is the abyss of all knowledge, that you may neither be deceived by the specious or high-sounding words of orators nor by the deceptive subtleties of philosophers. "Grow in grace and in the knowledge of Our Lord and Savior Jesus Christ." [9]

Now that we may all grow in grace and knowledge of Our Lord and Savior Jesus Christ, Eternal Wisdom, we shall speak of Him in the following chapters, after having made a distinction between the different kinds of wisdom.

13. Wisdom taken in general and according to the meaning of the word, is a "delectable knowledge"; [10] it is a taste for God and His truth.

There are several kinds of Wisdom. First there is *true* and *false* wisdom. True wisdom is fondness of truth, without guile or dissimulation. False wisdom is fondness of falsehood, disguised under the appearance of truth.

This *false* wisdom is the wisdom of the world, which according to the Holy Spirit is threefold: "Earthly, sensual and devilish wisdom." [11]

True wisdom is *natural* and *supernatural*. Natural wisdom is knowledge, in an eminent degree, of natural things in their principles; supernatural wisdom is knowledge of supernatural and divine things in their origin. This supernatural wisdom is divided into substantial or uncreated wisdom, and accidental or

4

created wisdom. *Accidental* and *created* wisdom is a share of Uncreated Wisdom communicated to men.[12] In other words, it is the gift of wisdom. *Substantial* or *Uncreated* Wisdom is the Son of God, Second Person of the Blessed Trinity; Eternal Wisdom in eternity, or Jesus Christ in the course of time. It is precisely of this Eternal Wisdom that we are now going to speak.

14. We shall contemplate Him *in eternity,* residing from His origin in the bosom of His Father as the object of His delight. We shall see Him *in time,* shining brightly in the creation of the universe. We shall behold Him in the deep humiliation of *His Incarnation and His mortal life.* We shall see Him glorious and triumphant in heaven. Finally, we shall speak of *the means* to possess and to keep Him.

To the philosophers, I leave their useless arguments; to the scientists, I leave the secrets of their worldly wisdom, for, "We speak wisdom among the perfect." [13]

To those seeking perfection, therefore, let us speak of True, Eternal, Uncreated and Incarnate Wisdom.

---

[1] Jeremias 11:23, 24; [2] Canticle 1:1; [3] Wisdom 8:16; [4] John 17:3; [5] Wisdom 15:3; [6] 1 Cor. 2:2; [7] Philip. 3:7; [8] Coloss. 2:4, 8; [9] 2 Peter 3:18; [10] St. Thomas, Pars. I. Qu. 45 Art. 5; [11] James 3:15; [12] St. Thomas, Pars II IIae Qu. 23 Art 2; [13] 1 Cor. 2:6.

CHAPTER TWO

The Origin and Excellence of Eternal Wisdom

15. Here we must exclaim with St. Paul: "O the depth and immensity, O the incomprehensibility of the Wisdom of God." [1] Who is the Angel so enlightened, who is the man so daring as to venture to explain adequately His origin? [2] Let all human eyes be closed that they may not be blinded by the glowing brightness of His radiance; let every tongue be silent for fear of tarnishing His perfect beauty in trying to reveal it; let every intelligence bow down and adore, lest, trying to fathom Him, it be oppressed by the immense glory of the Divine Wisdom.

16. The Holy Spirit, however, condescending to our weakness, gives us an idea of the excellence of Eternal Wisdom in the Book of Wisdom which He has caused to be written for us.

Eternal Wisdom, He tells us, "is a vapor of the power of God, and a certain emanation of the glory of the Almighty God; and, therefore, no defiled thing cometh unto Him, for He is the brightness of eternal light and the unspotted mirror of God's majesty and the image of His goodness." [3]

17. Divine Wisdom is the substantial and eternal concept of the beauty of God shown to St. John the

6

Evangelist in the wondrous ecstasy which he experienced on the Isle of Patmos, when he exclaimed: "In the beginning was the Word" (the Son of God, Eternal Wisdom) "and the Word was with God, and the Word was God." [4]

18. Of Him we read repeatedly in the Books of Solomon that Wisdom was created, that is to say, produced at the very beginning, before all creatures and before all time. He says of Himself "I was set up from all eternity, and of old before the earth was made. The depths were not yet and I was already conceived." [5]

19. In this sovereign beauty of His Wisdom, God the Father was well pleased in eternity and in time, as He distinctly assured us on the day of the baptism of His Son and at His Transfiguration: "This is My beloved Son in whom I am well pleased." [6]

The Apostles saw in His Transfiguration some radiation of that bright and incomprehensible beauty which filled them with delight and threw them into ecstasy. "We behold the Light radiant, sublime, immense, unlimited, older than heaven and chaos." [7] That is, in Eternal Wisdom we behold Him Who is illustrious, high, immense, infinite and older than the universe.

If I lack words to express even a very small idea which I have conceived of this beauty and sovereign delight—and my conception of them falls far short of the reality—who can have a right idea of them and explain them correctly? Only Thou, O great God, Who knowest what they are and canst reveal them to Whom Thou pleasest.

20. This is how, in the Twenty-fourth Chapter of Ecclesiasticus, Divine Wisdom Himself tells us the effects of His operation in our souls. I shall not comment upon them, lest by my feeble words I should diminish the splendor and sublimity of His words.

Wisdom shall praise her own self, and shall be honored in God, and shall glory in the midst of her people.

And shall open her mouth in the churches of the Most High, and shall glorify herself in the sight of His power.

And in the midst of her own people she shall be exalted, and shall be admired in the holy assembly.

And in the multitude of the elect she shall have praise. And among the blessed she shall be blessed, saying:

21. *I came out of the mouth of the Most High, the first born before all creatures.*

I made that in the heavens there should rise light that never faileth, and as a cloud I covered all the earth.

I dwelt in the highest places, and my throne is in the pillar of a cloud.

I alone have compassed the circuit of heaven, and

have penetrated into the bottom of the deep, and have walked in the ways of the sea.

And have stood in all the earth. And in every people.

22. *And in every nation I have had the chief rule.*

And by my power I have trodden under my feet the hearts of all the high and low: and in all these I sought rest, and I shall abide in the inheritance of the Lord.

23. *Then the Creator of all things commanded and said to me: and He that made me rested in my tabernacle.*

And He said to me: Let thy dwelling be in Jacob, and thy inheritance in Israel, and take root in My elect.

24. *From the beginning, and before the world, was I created, and unto the world to come I shall not cease to be: and in the holy dwelling place I have ministered before Him.*

And so was I established in Sion, and in the holy city likewise I rested: and my power was in Jerusalem.

25. *And I took root in an honorable people, and in the portion of my God His inheritance: and my abode is in the full assembly of saints.*

I was exalted like a cedar in Libanus, and as a cypress tree on Mount Sion.

I was exalted like a palm tree in Cades, and as a rose plant in Jericho.

LOVE OF ETERNAL WISDOM

As a fair olive tree in the plains, and as a plane-tree by the water in the streets, was I exalted.

I gave a sweet smell like cinnamon, and aromatical balm: I yielded a sweet odor like the best myrrh.

And I perfumed my dwelling like storax, and galbanum, and onyx, and aloes, and as the frankincense not cut: and my odor is as the purest balm.

I have stretched out my branches as the turpentine tree: and my branches are of honor and grace.

As the vine I have brought forth a pleasant odor: and my flowers are the fruit of honor and riches.

26. I am the mother of fair love, and of fear, and of knowledge, and of holy hope.

In me is all grace of the way and of the truth: in me is all hope of life and of virtue.

27. Come over to me, all ye that desire me: and be filled with my fruits.

For my spirit is sweet above honey: and my inheritance above honey and the honeycomb.

My memory is unto everlasting generations.

28. They that eat me shall yet hunger: and they that drink me shall yet thirst.

He that hearkeneth to me shall not be confounded: and they that work by me shall not sin.

They that explain me shall have life everlasting.

All these things are the book of life, and the covenant of the most High, and the knowledge of the truth.

29. All these trees and plants, to which Divine

Wisdom likens Himself, yielding as they do such various fruits, and being endowed as they are with such varied properties are figures of the great variety of states, occupations and virtues of the souls of men. Some of these souls resemble cedars by the loftiness of their hearts raised toward heaven; some resemble the cypress by their continual meditation on death; some resemble the palm tree by their humble endurance of labor; some resemble the rose tree by the shedding of their blood and their martyrdom; some, again, remind us of the plane tree planted by the waters, or of the terebinth with its wide spreading boughs, symbolizing the extent of their charity toward their brethren. And all these fragrant plants, like balm and myrrh and those others which are seen frequently, represent those retiring souls who are anxious to be better known to God than to their fellow man.

30. Having represented Himself as the parent and source of all that is good, Divine Wisdom now exhorts all men to forsake everything and to desire Him alone. St. Augustine tells us that He gives Himself to those only who wish to possess Him and who seek Him with all the zeal worthy of such a great treasure.

In verses 30 and 31 of the Twenty-fourth Chapter of Ecclesiasticus, Divine Wisdom indicates three degrees of piety, of which the last one is the perfect one:

1. To listen to God with humble submission.

2. To act in Him and by Him with persevering fidelity.

3. To obtain the necessary light and unction with which to inspire in others the love of Wisdom that will lead them to eternal life.

---

[1] Rom. 11:33;   [2] Isaias 53:8;   [3] Wisdom 7:25, 26;
[4] John 1:1;   [5] Prov. 8:23, 24;   [6] Matthew 3:17;
17:5;   [7] Hymn of Transfiguration.

CHAPTER THREE

*The Wonderful Power of Divine Wisdom in the
Creation of the World and of Man*

31. Eternal Wisdom began to manifest Himself
outside the bosom of His Father where He dwelt
from eternity, when He made light, heaven and
earth. St. John writes: "All things were made by the
Word," [1] that is to say, by Eternal Wisdom. Solomon
declares: "Wisdom is the parent and worker of all
things." [2]

Notice that he does not call Wisdom simply the
maker of the universe, but its parent, because the
maker does not love and maintain the object he has
made as does the parent his child.

32. When He had created all things the Eternal
Word dwelt in them "to contain, to sustain and to
renew all things." [3] This divine beauty, supremely
precise, has given to His creation the beautiful order
which we find in it. He has separated, arranged,
weighed, added and counted all that it contains. He
laid out the heavens, He placed the sun, the moon,
the stars and the planets in perfect order; He bal-
anced the foundations of the earth; He marked
boundaries and gave laws to the sea and the deep;
He established the mountains; He poised and bal-
anced even the fountains of water. In short, Divine
Wisdom Himself tells us: "I was with God ordering
all things, at once with such perfect accuracy and

such attractive variety that, as if at a game, I was playing to divert Myself and to divert My Father." [4]

33. This ineffable play of Divine Wisdom is apparent in the diversity of His creation. We see it in the angels, whose number is infinite; in the various characteristics of man; in the magnitude of the stars; in all the creatures with which He formed the universe. How admirable is the change of the seasons and of the weather! How great is the variety of instinct in the animals! How varied are the species of plants. How different the beauty of the flowers, the flavor of fruit! "Who is he who has received wisdom? Only he who has, will understand these mysteries of nature." [5]

34. Divine Wisdom has revealed all these things to the Saints, as we see from their lives. At times, upon seeing the beauty, the sweetness, and the order displayed by Eternal Wisdom in even His smallest creatures, such as a bee, an ant, an ear of corn, a flower, a little worm, they became wrapt in ecstasy.

35. If the power of Eternal Wisdom is so manifest in the beauty and order of the universe, then His greatness shines forth still more brilliantly in the creation of man who is a Divine masterpiece, the living image of His own beauty and perfections, the great vessel of His graces, the admirable treasury of His riches, and His sole representative on earth. "And by Thy wisdom hast appointed man, that he should

have dominion over the creature that was made by Thee." [6]

36. Here I should expound, to the glory of this magnificent and powerful Worker, the original beauty and excellence which man received from Him when He created him; but the blemish of the heinous sin which man committed has fallen upon me, miserable child of Eve, and has so benighted my intellect that I can speak of the original state of man but imperfectly.

37. He made copies, so to speak, of the brilliant expressions of His intellect, His memory, His will, and gave them to the soul of man so that he would be the living image of Divinity; He kindled in his heart the fire of pure love of God; He gave him a glorious body, and summarized in him all the various perfections of the Angels, the animals, and other creatures.

38. In man everything was bright without a shadow, beautiful without ugliness, pure without stain, well-ordered without disturbance—all without blemish or imperfection. He was endowed with the light of wisdom in his mind, which gave him a perfect knowledge of the Creator and His creatures. The grace of God was in his soul, causing him to be innocent and pleasing to the most High. His body was immortal. In his heart, free from the fear of death, there was the pure love of God. He loved God solely for Himself and without abatement. In short, man

was so perfect he was continually enraptured by God and abode in Him, without passions to conquer, without enemies to fight. O the liberality of Eternal Wisdom to man! O the happy state of man in his innocence!

39. But, O greatest of all misfortunes! Behold this magnificent vessel breaks into a thousand pieces; this beautiful star falls; this resplendent sun becomes covered with spots. Man sins, and by sinning, he loses his wisdom, his innocence, his beauty, his immortality. In a word, he loses all that he had received and becomes a prey to every evil. He becomes dull-witted, dark of soul, and blind. His heart has turned cold toward God; he does not love Him any more. His soul, blackened with sin, resembles the devil. His passions have become unruly; he is no longer their master. The devils are his partners; he is their abode and also their slave. Even the ordinary creatures attack him and war against him. Behold man suddenly become the slave of the devil, the object of the wrath of God, the prey of hell!

In his own sight, man appears so horrid that he is ashamed of himself and hides. He is cursed and condemned to death. He is driven out of his earthly paradise and has no longer a place in heaven. He is without hope of being happy and must live a wretched life on this accursed earth. He must die a criminal. After his death, he must be as a devil, damned for ever in body and soul, and his curse descends upon his children.

Such is the frightful woe man brought upon himself by sinning. Such is the equitable sentence which the justice of God pronounced against him.

40. In this state Adam is, as it were, without hope. Neither the Angels nor any other creature can save him. Nothing can restore him, for he was too beautiful and too well made in his creation, and now, because of his sin, he is too hideous and too defiled. He finds himself driven away from paradise and from the presence of God. He feels the justice of God pursuing him and all his posterity. He sees heaven closed and nobody to open it. He sees hell open, and nobody to close it.

[1] John 1:3;   [2] Wisdom 7:12, 21;   [3] Wisdom 1:7; 7:27;   [4] Prov. 8:30, 31;   [5] Ps. 106:43;   [6] Wisdom 9:2;   [7] St. Gregory Hom. 29 in Evan.

CHAPTER FOUR

The Wonderful Goodness and Mercy of Eternal Wisdom before His Incarnation

41. Eternal Wisdom is keenly moved by the predicament of the unfortunate Adam and all his descendants. Deeply grieved, He beholds His vessel of honor broken, His image defaced, His masterpiece ruined, His representative on earth overthrown. He listens tenderly to his groans and wails. He is moved with compassion upon seeing the sweat of his brow, the tears in his eyes, the labor of his arms, the sorrow of his heart and the affliction of his soul.

42. It seems to me that this amiable Prince now calls to council for a second time the Blessed Trinity, for man's restoration, as He had already done for his creation. In this grand council there seems to be taking place a kind of contest between Eternal Wisdom and the justice of God.

43. I seem to hear Eternal Wisdom pleading the cause of man and saying that on account of his sin, he and his descendants rightly deserve to be damned for all eternity with the rebel angels; but that mercy should be shown to him because he sinned by weakness and ignorance rather than through malice. On the one hand, He points out that it would be a great pity were such a perfect masterpiece to remain for ever the slave of the devil, and were millions and millions of men to be lost on account of the sin of

one man. On the other hand, He shows how appropriate it would be to fill those places in heaven left vacant by the fall of the rebel angels, and what great glory it would give to God, both in time and in eternity, were man to be saved.

44. I seem to hear the justice of God replying that the sentence of death and eternal damnation is pronounced against man and his posterity, and that it must be executed without pardon or mercy, as it was in the case of Lucifer and his followers; that man has shown himself ungrateful for the favors received, that he followed the example of Satan's disobedience and pride, and therefore must follow him in his punishment.

45. Eternal Wisdom, seeing that there is nothing in the whole of creation capable of atoning for the sin of man, of satisfying divine justice and appeasing the wrath of God, and, nevertheless, wishing to save man whom He loves, Himself finds an admirable means of doing so. Drawn by an unheard of and incomprehensible excess of love, this lovable and sovereign Prince offers Himself in sacrifice to His Father in order to satisfy Divine justice, to calm Divine anger, and to redeem us from the slavery of the devil and the flames of hell, and to merit for us eternal happiness.

46. His offer is accepted. A decision is reached and adopted: Eternal Wisdom, the Son of God, will become Man at the appropriate time and in pre-

ordained circumstances. During the ages which elapsed from the creation of the world and the sin of Adam until the Incarnation of Divine Wisdom, Adam and his descendants died, according to the law enacted by God. But, in prevision of the Incarnation of the Son of God, Adam's descendants received the necessary grace to obey His commandments and to do worthy penance for their transgression. If they died in the grace and friendship of God their souls went to Limbo, there to wait for their Savior and Liberator to open to them the gates of heaven.

47. During the time that elapsed before His Incarnation, Eternal Wisdom gave proof to man in a thousand ways of His friendship for them, and of His great desire to grant them His favors and to converse with them. "My delight," He said, "is to be with the children of men." [1] "He went about seeking such as were worthy of Him." [2] That is, He gave Himself to those who were worthy of His friendship, worthy of His treasures, worthy of Himself. "Through different nations He conveyed Himself to holy souls to make them friends of God and prophets. He alone has formed all the holy Patriarchs, the friends of God, the Prophets and the Saints of the Old and New Testament." [3]

This Eternal Wisdom inspired the men of God; He spoke by the mouths of the Prophets; He guided them in their ways, and enlightened them in their doubts, sustained them in their weaknesses and delivered them from evil.

48. This is how the Holy Spirit Himself relates it all in Chapter Ten of the Book of Wisdom:

She (Wisdom) preserved him (Adam) who was first formed by God, the Father of the world, when he was created alone.

And she brought him out of his sin, and gave him power to govern all things.

But when the unjust went away from her in his anger, (Cain) he perished by the fury wherewith he murdered his brother.

For whose cause, when water destroyed the earth, Wisdom healed it again, directing the course of the just (Noah) by contemptible wood.

Moreover when the nations had conspired together to consent to wickedness, she knew the just (Abraham) and preserved him without blame to God, and kept him strong against the compassion of his son (Isaac).

She delivered the just man (Lot) who fled from the wicked that were perishing, when the fire came down upon Pentapolis,

Whose land for a testimony of their wickedness is desolate and smoketh to this day, and the trees bear fruits that ripen not, and a standing pillar of salt is a monument of an incredulous soul (Lot's wife).

For regarding not Wisdom, they did not only slip in this that they were ignorant of good things, but they left also unto men a memorial of their folly, so that in the things in which they sinned, they could not so much as lie hid.

49. But Wisdom hath delivered from sorrow them that attend upon her.

She conducted the just, (Jacob) when he fled from his brother's wrath through the right ways, and showed him the kingdom of God, and gave him the knowledge of the holy things, made him honorable in his labors, and accomplished his labors.

In the deceit of them that overreached him, she stood by him and made him honorable.

She kept him safe from his enemies, and she defended him from seducers, and gave him a strong conflict, that he might overcome and know that Wisdom is mightier than all.

She forsook not the just (Joseph) when he was sold, but delivered him from sinners. She went down with him into the pit.

And in bands she left him not, till she brought him the succor of the kingdom, and power against those that oppressed him: and showed them to be liars that had accused him, and gave him everlasting glory.

She delivered the just people (the Hebrews) and blameless seed from the nations that oppressed them.

She entered into the soul of the servant of God

(Moses) and stood against dreadful kings in wonders and signs.

And she rendered to the just the wages of their labors and conducted them in a wonderful way: and she was to them for a covert by day and for the light of stars by night:

And she brought them through the Red Sea and carried them over to a great water.

But their enemies she drowned in the sea, and from the depth of hell she brought them out. Therefore the just took the spoils of the wicked.

And they sung to Thy holy name, O Lord: and they praised with one accord Thy victorious hand.

For Wisdom opened the mouth of the dumb and made the tongues of infants eloquent.

50. In the next Chapter of the Book of Wisdom the Holy Spirit recounts the different evils from which Eternal Wisdom delivered Moses and the Israelites while they sojourned in the desert. To this recounting may be added all those who were delivered and preserved by Eternal Wisdom from great evil under the Old and New Testaments, such as Daniel from the lion's den; Susanna from the false crime of which she was accused; the three children from the furnace of Babylon; St. Peter from prison; St. John from the cauldron of boiling oil; and number-less martyrs and confessors from the torments to which their bodies were subjected, and from the calumnies which blackened their good name. "By

wisdom they were healed, whoever have pleased thee, O Lord, from the beginning." [4]

51. Let us exclaim then: A thousand times happy is the man into whose soul Wisdom has come to dwell! In whatever battles he has to wage he will be victorious; from whatever dangers threaten him he will escape; in whatever sorrows afflict him he will have joy and comfort; and through whatever humiliations he passes, he will be exalted and glorified in time and in eternity.

[1] Prov. 8:34;   [2] Wisdom 6:17;   [3] Wisdom 7:27;
[4] Wisdom 9:19.

CHAPTER FIVE

The Wonderful Excellence of Eternal Wisdom

52. As the Holy Spirit has deigned to show us the excellence of Eternal Wisdom in Chapter Eight of the Book of Wisdom, in such clear and sublime words, it will suffice to quote from Holy Scripture with only a few remarks.

53. *"Wisdom reacheth therefore from end to end mightily, and ordereth all things sweetly."* Nothing is so sweet as Wisdom. He is meek in Himself without any bitterness. He is meek in those who love Him, never causing them weariness. He is meek in His ways of acting, never resorting to violence. He is so discreet and gentle that you might often think He is absent from the misfortunes and reverses that take place. But as His power is unconquerable He acts imperceptibly, yet strongly, to make all things reach their end by means not known to man. The wise man should, after His example, act strongly with gentleness, and gently with strength.

54. *"I have loved and sought out Wisdom from my youth, and have desired to take her for my spouse."* Whosoever wishes to acquire the great treasure of Wisdom, must, after the example of Solomon, seek for that treasure;

1. *Early*, even, if possible, in his youth. 2. *Spiritually*, that is, purely as a chaste spouse looks for his bride. 3. *Steadfastly*, perseveringly till he has

found Wisdom. It is certain that Eternal Wisdom loves our souls so much as to espouse them, and He goes so far as to contract with them a spiritual but true marriage which the world knows not, but of which history supplies us with examples.

55. "*She glorifieth her nobility by being conversant with God, yea and the Lord of all things hath loved her.*" Wisdom is true God. Behold the glory of His origin. God the Father is well pleased in Him, as He has testified. Behold how He is loved.

56. "*For it is Wisdom that teacheth the knowledge of God, and is the chooser of His works.*" Eternal Wisdom alone enlighteneth every man that cometh into the world; He alone has come down from heaven to teach the secrets of God, and we have no other true Master but the Incarnate Wisdom whose name is Jesus Christ. He alone directs to their end all the works of God, more particularly the saints, teaching them to appreciate and practice what He has taught them.

57. "*If riches be desired in life, what is richer than Wisdom that maketh all things? And if sense do work, who is a more artful worker than she of those things that are? If a man loves justice, his labors have great virtue; for she teacheth temperance and prudence and justice and fortitude, which are such things as men can have nothing more profitable in life,*" By these words Solomon shows that as we must love only Eternal Wisdom, so it is also from

Him that we can expect to receive all material goods, knowledge of the secrets of nature, all spiritual goods, and the theological and cardinal virtues.

58. *"And if a man desire much knowledge; she knoweth things past, and judgeth of all things to come; she knoweth the subtleties of speeches and the solutions of arguments; she knoweth signs and wonders before they are done, and the events of times and ages."* Whosoever wishes to obtain such knowledge of spiritual and natural things as is not common, dry and superficial, but above the ordinary, holy and solid, must make every effort to acquire Wisdom—for without Wisdom man is reputed as nothing before God, though he may pass as learned before men. "He shall be nothing regarded." [1]

59. *I purposed therefore to take her to live with me; knowing that she will communicate to me of her good things, and will be a comfort in my cares and griefs.* Who can be poor, with this Wisdom so rich and munificent? Who can grieve when in possession of that Wisdom so gentle, so charming, so loving? And yet, who, of all those who seek this Wisdom, can sincerely say with Solomon: "I purposed therefore." Most have not made that resolution sincerely; they have but a slight desire, or take but wavering and undetermined resolutions. This is the reason they never find Wisdom.

60. *For her sake I shall have glory among the*

multitudes and honor with the ancients, though I be young.

And I shall be found of quick conceit in judgment, and shall be admired in the sight of the mighty, and the faces of princes shall wonder at me.

They shall wait for me when I hold my peace and they shall look upon me when I speak, and if I talk much they shall lay their hands on their mouths.

Moreover by means of her I shall have immortality; and shall leave behind me an everlasting memory to them that come after me.

I shall set the people in order; and nations shall be subject to me.

St. Gregory, commenting upon these words of the wise man praising himself, remarks that those whom God has chosen to write Holy Scripture are filled with the Holy Spirit; they, as it were, go out of themselves and enter Him Who possesses them, and thus being the mouthpieces of God, they consider Him alone in what they say; they speak of themselves as though of another.

61. *Terrible kings hearing shall be afraid of me; among the multitude I shall be found good and valiant in war.*

When I go into my house I shall repose myself with her, for her conversation hath no bitterness, nor her company any tediousness, but joy and gladness.

Thinking these things with myself, and pondering

28

them in my heart, that to be allied with Wisdom is immortality.

And there is great delight in her friendship, and inexhaustible riches in the works of her hands, and in the exercise of conference with her, wisdom and glory in the communication of her words; I went about seeking that I might take her to myself.

The wise man after summarizing, draws this conclusion: "I went about seeking her."

To acquire Eternal Wisdom we must seek Him ardently, that is, we must be willing to abandon all, to suffer all, and to undertake all things in order to possess Him. There are but few who find Him because there are but few who seek Him in a manner worthy of Him.

62. In Chapter Seven also of the Book of Wisdom, the Holy Spirit speaks of the excellence of Wisdom, in the following terms: *in Wisdom "is the spirit of understanding; wholly, one, manifold, subtle, eloquent, active, undefiled, sure, sweet, loving that which is good, quick, which nothing hindereth, beneficent, gentle, kind, steadfast, assured, secure, having all power, overseeing all things, and containing all spirits, intelligible, pure, subtle, for Wisdom is more active than all active things; and reacheth everywhere by reason of her purity."* [2]

"Wisdom is an infinite treasure to men, which they that use become the friends of God, being commended for the gift of discipline." [3]

63. What man, having read these powerful and tender words of the Holy Spirit expressing the beauty, the excellence and the treasures of Eternal Wisdom, will not love Him and seek Him with all his strength; the more so as He is an infinite treasure, proper to man, because man is made for Him; and because He himself is infinitely desirous of communicating Himself to man?

[1] Wisdom 3:17;   [2] Wisdom 7:22, 23, 24;   [3] Wisdom 7:14.

Chapter Six

The Eager Desire of Divine Wisdom to Communicate Himself to Man

64. The bond of friendship between Eternal Wisdom and man is so close as to be incomprehensible. WISDOM IS FOR MAN, AND MAN IS FOR WISDOM. "He is an infinite treasure to man," [1] and not to the Angels nor to any other creature.

The reason for this affection of Eternal Wisdom for man, is that in creation man is the summary of all His wonders; he is His little and His great world, His living image, His representative on earth. And from the moment when, out of His exceeding love for man, Divine Wisdom became like unto him by assuming human nature, and died to redeem him, man is loved by Divine Wisdom as a brother, a friend, a disciple, a pupil. Man is the price of His blood, and the co-heir to His kingdom. So much so, that infinite violence is done to Him when man either refuses to give Him his heart or wrests it from Him.

65. The longings of this eternal and supremely lovable Beauty for the friendship of man are so intense that He has purposely composed a Book, disclosing therein His excellences and His desires to capture that friendship. This Book is the Canticle of Canticles. It reads like a love song composed by a suitor to win the affection of his beloved. His long-

ing for the heart of man, expressed therein, is so tender; His pursuit of man's friendship so eager; His appeals and wishes are so loving, that on hearing Him you might think that He is not the Sovereign of heaven and earth and that without man He cannot be happy.

66. Sometimes in search of man, He travels the highways; at other times, He climbs the peaks of the highest mountains; now, He is at the gates of the cities; now, He enters into the public places and the assemblies of men, where, we may believe, He might cry out: "Ye men, ye children of men; it is to you I appeal, you I wish for, you I seek, you I claim. Hear ye and come to Me; I will make you happy." [1a]

And to draw you irresistibly He may say: "By Me and My grace, kings reign, princes rule, and mighty monarchs wear their crowns and carry their scepters. I inspire legislators with their knowledge to establish good laws for the governing of state. I give strength to magistrates to administer justice fairly and fearlessly."

67. In the Book of Proverbs, Eternal Wisdom declares: "*I love them that love Me, and they that in the morning early watch for Me shall find Me.*" [2] Continuing His search for man the Holy Spirit tells us that if we respond to His search we shall find abundance of all goods, for with Him are riches and glory, honor and dignity, lasting pleasure and true

virtue, and it is incomparably better for a man to possess Him than to possess all the gold and silver of the world, all the precious stones and the jewels of the universe.

Those who go to Him are led by the paths of justice and prudence. He enriches them with the possession of true children, to the satiation of their desires. They are persuaded that His greatest pleasure and fondest delight is to converse and to dwell with the children of men.

68. *"Now therefore, ye children, hear Me; blessed are they that keep My ways. Hear instruction and be wise, and refuse it not. Blessed is the man that heareth Me, and that watcheth daily at My gates and waiteth at the posts of My doors. He that shall find Me shall find Life, and shall have salvation from the Lord, but he that shall sin against Me shall hurt his own soul. All that hate Me love death."* [3]

69. After all these most tender and engaging words to win man's friendship, Eternal Wisdom still fears that because of His infinite splendor and sovereign majesty some will not dare to approach Him, out of respect. Therefore, He now tells them that Wisdom is easy of access; *"is easily seen by them that love her; she preventeth them that covet her, so that she first sheweth herself unto them; and he that awaketh early to seek her shall not labor,"* to find Him, *"for he shall find her sitting at his door,"* [4] waiting for him.

70. Lastly, Eternal Wisdom, to be nearer to man and to show him His love in a more touching manner, went so far as to make Himself Man, so far as to become a child, to be poor and to die on the Cross for His own creatures. We know how repeatedly He pleaded, while on earth, to be accepted by man. We can imagine how He would speak to us now: "Come all ye to Me; it is I, do not fear; why are you afraid? I am like unto you; I love you. Do you fear because you are sinners? But it is sinners I am seeking; I am the friend of sinners. Or is it because through your own fault you have strayed from the fold? But I am the Good Shepherd. Is it finally, because you are weighed down by your sins, covered with filth and burdened with sadness? Ah, but that is precisely a reason for coming to Me, because I will refresh and comfort you."

71. As, on the one hand, He wishes to show His love for man by dying to save him; and as, on the other hand, He cannot decide to leave man, He devises the admirable secret of dying and leaving while abiding with man forever in the loving mystery of the Holy Eucharist. To succeed in satisfying His love in this mystery He does not hesitate to change and reverse the laws of nature. He does not hide Himself under a brilliant diamond or other precious stone because He does not wish to dwell merely exteriorly with man; but, He hides Himself under the appearances of a morsel of bread, which is the

staple food of man, so that being received by man He may dwell also in his heart, and there take His delight. "O Eternal Wisdom!" says a holy man, "O God truly lavish of Himself in His desire to be with man!"

72. How obdurate and ungrateful we must be if we are not moved by the ardent longings, the loving pursuits and friendly tokens of this endearing Wisdom! But what is our callousness; what will be our chastisement, even in this world, if, instead of listening to Him, we turn a deaf ear to Him; if instead of seeking Him we flee from Him; if instead of honoring and loving Him, we despise and offend Him! *Those who did not regard Wisdom,"* the Holy Spirit tells us, *"did not only slip in this that they were ignorant of good things, but they left also to men a memorial of their folly, so that in the things in which they sinned, they could not so much as lie hid."* [5]

Threefold is the misfortune, during life, of those who do not take the trouble to acquire Wisdom. They fall: 1, into ignorance and blindness; 2, into foolishness; 3, into scandal and sin.

But what will be their misfortune at the moment of death, when, despite themselves, they will hear the reproachful words of Wisdom: *"I have called you and you have not made answer"?* [6] I have held out my arms to you and you have scorned me; I have waited for you sitting at your door, and you have not heeded me. *"I also will laugh in your destruction, and will mock;"* [7] I will have no ears to listen to

35

your wails; no eyes to see your tears; no heart to be moved by your bitter sobbing; no hands to come to your assistance.

But what will be their misfortune in hell? Read what the Holy Spirit Himself tells us of the misfortune, the wailing, the repining and the despair of these foolish souls in hell, realizing, when it is too late, their folly and the calamity of having rejected the Wisdom of God. *"Such things as these the sinners said in hell."* [8] They begin to speak wisely when they are in hell.

73. Let us, then, long for Divine Wisdom and seek Him alone. Moreover, let us remember that all things desirable are not to be compared with Wisdom. We can desire nothing better than Wisdom. Hence, whatever gifts of God, whatever heavenly treasures you wish for, if your desire does not include Wisdom, you are wishing for something of less value than Wisdom. Ah, if we knew the infinite Treasure of Wisdom laid up for us—and I admit that what I have said of Wisdom is as nothing—we would be longing for that Treasure day and night; we would run to the ends of the world; we would cheerfully pass through fire and sword, if that were necessary, to earn that Treasure.

But we must be beware of being mistaken in our choice, for there are several kinds of wisdom.

[1] Wisdom 7:14;   [1a] Prov. 8:4;   [2] Prov. 8:17;
[3] Prov. 8:32-36;   [4] Wisdom 6:12, 13;   [5] Wisdom 10:88;   [6] Prov. 1:24;   [7] Prov. 1:26;   [8] Wisdom 5:14.

Chapter Seven

The Choice of True Wisdom

74. There is the Wisdom of God, the only true Wisdom that deserves to be loved as a great Treasure.

There is also the wisdom of the corrupt world which must be condemned and detested as evil and pernicious.

Moreover, there is the wisdom of the philosophers which we must despise when it is not true philosophy, and because it is often dangerous to salvation.

So far, following the advice of St. Paul, we have spoken of the Wisdom of God to chosen souls, but lest they should be deceived by the false luster of worldly wisdom, let us expose its deceit and malice.

75. The wisdom of the world is that of which it is written: "I will destroy the wisdom of the wise" [1] according to the world. "The wisdom of the flesh is an enemy to God." [2] "This is not the wisdom descending from above but earthly, sensual, devilish." [3]

This worldly wisdom consists in the exact compliance with the maxims and the fashions of the world; in a continuous trend toward greatness and esteem. It is a secret and unceasing pursuit of pleasures and personal interests, not in a gross and open manner so as to cause scandal, but in a secret, deceitful and scheming fashion. Otherwise, it would not be what the world calls wisdom, but rank licentiousness.

76. Those who proceed according to the wisdom of the world are those who know how to manage well their affairs and to arrange things to their temporal advantage without appearing to do so; who know the art of deceiving and how to cleverly cheat without being noticed; who say or do one thing and have another thing in mind; who are thoroughly acquainted with the way and the flattery of the world; who know how to please everybody in order to reach their goal, not troubling much about the honor and interests of God; who make a secret but deadly fusion of truth with untruth, of the Gospel with the world, of virtue with vice, of Jesus Christ with Satan; who wish to pass as honest people but not as religious men; who despise and corrupt or readily condemn every religious practice which does not conform to their own. In short, the worldly-wise are those who, being guided only by their human senses and reason, seek only to appear as Christian and honest folk, without troubling much to please God or to do penance for the sins which they have committed against His divine Majesty.

77. The worldling bases his conduct upon his honor, upon what people say, upon convention, upon good cheer, upon personal interest, upon refined manners, upon witty jokes. These are the seven inno-

cent incentives, so he thinks, upon which he can rely that he may lead an easy life.

He has virtues of his own for which he is canonized by the world. These are manliness, finesse, diplomacy, tact, gallantry, politeness, sprightliness. He considers as serious sins such traits as lack of feeling, silliness, dullness, sanctimoniousness.

78. He adheres as strictly as possible to the commandments which the world has given him:

1. Thou shalt be well acquainted with the world.
2. Thou shalt be an "honest" man.
3. Thou shalt be successful in business.
4. Thou shalt keep what is thine.
5. Thou shalt get on in the world.
6. Thou shalt make friends.
7. Thou shalt be a society man.
8. Thou shalt make merry.
9. Thou shalt not be a killjoy.
10. Thou shalt avoid singularity, dullness and an air of piety.

79. Never was the world so corrupt as it is now, because it was never so astute, so wise in its own conceit, so cunning. It is so skillful in deceiving the soul seeking perfection that it makes use of truth to foster untruth, of virtue to authorize vice and it even distorts the meaning of Christ's own truths to give authority to its own maxims. "The number of those who are fools according to God, is infinite." [4]

LOVE OF ETERNAL WISDOM

80. The *earthly wisdom* spoken of by St. James is an excessive striving for worldly goods. The worldly-wise make a secret profession of this type of wisdom when they allow themselves to become attached to their earthly possessions, when they strive to become rich, when they go to law and bring useless actions against others in order to acquire or to keep temporal goods; when their every thought, word and deed is mainly directed toward obtaining or retaining something temporal. As to working out their eternal salvation and making use of the means to do so, such as reception of the Sacraments and prayer, they accomplish these duties only carelessly, in a very off-hand manner, once in a while, and for the sake of appearances.

81. *Sensual wisdom* is a lustful desire for pleasure. The worldly-wise make a profession of it when they seek only the satisfaction of the senses; when they are inordinately fond of entertainment; when they shun whatever mortifies and inconveniences the body, such as fasting and other austerities; when they continually think of eating, drinking, playing, laughing, amusing themselves and having an agreeable time; when they eagerly seek after soft beds, merry games, sumptuous feasts and fashionable society. Then, after having unscrupulously indulged in all these pleasures—perhaps without displeasing the world or injuring their health—they look for "the least scrupulous" confessor (such is the name théy

give to those easygoing confessors who shirk their duty) that they may receive from him, at little cost, the peaceful sanction of their soft and effeminate life, and a plenary indulgence for all their sins. I say, at little cost, for these sensually wise want as penance the recitation of only a few prayers, or the giving of an alms, because they dislike what afflicts the body.

82. *Devilish wisdom* consists in an unlawful striving for human esteem and honors. This is the wisdom which the worldly-wise profess when they aim, although not openly, at greatness, honors, dignities and high positions; when they wish to be seen, esteemed, praised and applauded by men; when in their studies, their works, their endeavors their words and actions, they seek only the good opinion and praise of men so that they may be looked upon as pious people, as men of learning, as great leaders, as clever lawyers, as people of boundless and distinguished merit, or deserving of high consideration; while they cannot bear an insult or a rebuke; or they cover up their faults and make a show of their fine qualities.

83. With Our Lord Jesus Christ, the Incarnate Wisdom, we must detest and condemn these three kinds of false wisdom if we wish to acquire the true one which does not seek its own interest, which is not found on this earth nor in the heart of those who lead a comfortable life, but which abhors all

that which is great and high in the estimation of men.

84. In addition to the earthly wisdom which is pernicious and to be condemned there is the natural wisdom of philosophers. This wisdom was eagerly sought after by the Egyptians and the Greeks; "The Greeks seek after wisdom." [5] Those among them who had acquired it were called Magi or Wise Men. This wisdom is an eminent knowledge of nature and its elements. It was given in full to Adam, in his innocence; it was abundantly bestowed upon Solomon, and, after him, several great men have shared it, as history testifies.

85. Philosophers boast of their philosophical reasoning as being the means to acquire this wisdom. Scientists boast of the secrets in which they imagine this natural wisdom is to be found.

86. It is true that Scholastic Philosophy when studied in a Christian spirit develops the mind and enables it to understand the higher sciences, but it will never bring us to the so-called natural wisdom so much renowned in antiquity.

87. The true scientist realizes that his ability is a gift of God and that he must prove himself worthy of it by dedicated Christian labor and prayer.

88. True science must always seek to honor Jesus Christ, Incarnate Wisdom, in whom are all the treasures of the wisdom and knowledge of God, all the ties of nature, of grace and glory. The scientist must

obey the Holy Spirit, Who warns him: "Seek not the things that are too high for thee." [6]

89. Let us, therefore, remain with Jesus Christ, Eternal Wisdom. Away from Him there is but wandering, untruth and death. "I am the way, the truth and the life." [7]

Let us now see the effects of Eternal Wisdom in our souls.

[1] 1 Cor. 1:19; [2] Rom. 8:7; [3] James 3:15; [4] Eccles. 1:15; [5] 1 Cor., 1:22; [6] Eccles. 3:22; [7] John 14:6.

Chapter Eight

The Wonderful Effects of Eternal Wisdom in the Souls of Those Who Possess Him

90. The greatest delight of this sovereign Beauty —loving by nature that "which is good," [1] and more in particular the good of man—is to diffuse Himself. Hence, the Holy Spirit tells us that Wisdom looks among the nations for worthy people and "conveyeth herself into holy souls;" [2] and it is by this communication of Eternal Wisdom that the friends of God and the Prophets are made.

Formerly, He entered into the soul of Moses, the servant of God, and communicated to him abundant light to understand great things, and a wonderful power to work miracles and to obtain victories. "She entered into the soul of the servant of God and stood against dreadful kings in wonders and signs." [3]

When Divine Wisdom enters into a soul He brings to it a variety and an abundance of good things, and imparts to it innumerable riches; "All good things came to me together with her, and innumerable riches through her hands." [4] Such is Solomon's testimony to the truth after he had received wisdom.

91. Among the many effects produced in our souls by Divine Wisdom—which often remain so hidden that we do not perceive them—we will point out some of the most usual.

92. 1. Eternal Wisdom communicates to the

soul that possesses Him His all-enlightening spirit; "I wished and understanding was given to me; I called and the spirit of understanding came upon me." [5] This subtle and penetrating spirit causes man, after the example of Solomon, to judge all things with great discernment and a keen intelligence. On account of the wisdom which has been communicated by my mind, "I shall be found of quick conceit in judgment, and shall be admired in the sight of the mighty." [5a]

93. He communicates to man the great science of the saints, and also natural sciences, even of the most mysterious, when such knowledge is expedient for them. "If a man desire much knowledge, she knoweth things past and judgeth of things to come: she knoweth the subtleties of speeches and the solutions of arguments." [6]

To Jacob He gave the science of the saints. [7]

To Solomon He gave the true knowledge of our nature. [8] He disclosed to him many secrets which nobody had known before him. [9]

94. From this unbounded source of light the great Doctors of the Church, notably St. Thomas, as he himself confesses, have drawn the wonderful learning which made them so worthy of commendation. You will notice that the gifts of light and knowledge given by Divine Wisdom are not dull, barren and void of piety, but enlightening, full of unction and conducive to activity and holiness; they move the

45

heart and satisfy it while they illuminate the mind.

95. 2. Wisdom not only gives man a light to know the truth, but also a wonderful capacity for making truth known to others. "Wisdom has knowledge of the voice." [10]

Wisdom knows what is to be said, and He communicates the talent to say it well, for "He opened the mouth of the dumb and made the tongues of infants eloquent." [11]

He loosened Moses' tongue which had an impediment.[12] He put His words in the mouths of the Prophets "to root up and to pull down, to waste and to destroy, to build and to plant"; [13] though they admitted that of themselves they could not speak better than children. He gave the Apostles fluent facility to preach the Gospel everywhere and to proclaim the wonderful works of God; "He made their mouth rich with words." [14]

As Divine Wisdom is the Word of God in eternity as well as in time, He has always spoken, and by His word all things were made and restored. He spoke by the Prophets and Apostles, and He will speak until the consummation of the world, by the mouth of those to whom He will communicate Himself.

96. But the words which the Divine Wisdom communicates are not common, natural and human words, they are the words of God.[15] They are strong, effective, piercing words; "more piercing than any

46

two-edged sword"; [16] shooting forth from the heart of him by whom He speaks and penetrating the heart of him who hears them. This was the gift of wisdom which Solomon had received, he tells us: "God has given me to speak according to the feelings of my heart." [17]

97. These are the words which Our Lord promised the Apostles when He said: "I will give you a mouth and wisdom which your adversaries will not be able to resist." [18]

O how few are the preachers today who possess this ineffable gift of eloquence and who can say with St. Paul: "We speak the wisdom of God." [19] Most of them speak from the natural knowledge of their intellect, or from what they have borrowed from books; not from the love which Divine Wisdom has put into their hearts; nor from the divine abundance which Wisdom has communicated to them.[20] Hence it is that now we hear of so few conversions brought about by preaching. If a preacher had truly received from Wisdom this gift of eloquence, his listeners could have scarcely resisted his words any more than could have those who listened to Eternal Wisdom speaking through the mouth of St. Stephen. "Those who listened were not able to resist the wisdom and the spirit that spoke." [21] Such a speaker would speak with so much unction and authority, that his words would not become empty or unavailing.

98. 3. Eternal Wisdom, Who is the object of the joy and satisfaction of the Eternal Father, and the delight of the Angels, is also to the man who possesses Him the source of the purest joys and consolation. He gives that man a relish for the things of God, and makes him lose a desire for things created. He enlightens his mind with the brightness of His divine light. He pours into his heart ineffable joy, sweetness and peace, even in the midst of the hardest trials and tribulations, as St. Paul bears witness when he exclaims: "I exceedingly abound with joy in all my tribulations." [22] Solomon proclaims: "When I go into my house, although I am by myself, I shall repose myself with her, for her conversation has no bitterness, nor her company any tediousness, but joy and gladness." [23] And not only do I find joy, being with Him in my house and in my conversation with Him, but in every place and in all things, for Wisdom "went before me." [24] "There is great delight in her friendship"; [25] whilst the pleasures and the joy found in creatures have but semblance of pleasure, and are affliction of the mind.

99. When Eternal Wisdom communicates Himself to a soul He confers upon it the gifts of the Holy Spirit and all the great virtues in an eminent degree. That is, He bestows the theological virtues: faith, hope, charity; the cardinal virtues: temperance, prudence, justice, fortitude; moral vir-

tues, such as: religion, humility, meekness, obedience, detachment, mortification, prayer. These, and other admirable virtues are the heavenly gifts which the Holy Spirit describes divinely in but a few words: "If a man love justice; her labors have great virtues, for she teacheth temperance and prudence, and justice and fortitude, which are such things as man can have nothing more profitable in life." [26]

100. Lastly, as Eternal Wisdom is "more active than all active things," [27] He does not allow those who enjoy His friendship to languish in sloth and negligence. He sets them on fire and makes them do great things for the glory of God and the salvation of souls. To prove them and make them worthy of Him, He gives them occasion for great combats and keeps in store for them contradictions and crosses in almost everything they undertake. He allows the devil to tempt them, the world to calumniate and abuse them, their enemies to have the upper hand and to crush them, their friends and relatives to forsake and betray them. Sometimes, He will cause them to suffer the loss of their goods or of their health; at other times He will load them with reproach, sadness and despondency. In a word, He will try them variously in the crucible of tribulation "but," the Holy Spirit reminds us, "afflicted in few things, in many they shall be rewarded, because God has tried them and found them worthy of Himself. As gold in the furnace He has

proved them; and as a victim of a holocaust He has received them; and in time there shall be respect had to them." [28]

"Wisdom has made the just honorable in his labors, and accomplished his labors. In the deceit of them that over-reached him she stood by him and made him honorable. She kept him safe from his enemies and she defended him from seducers, and gave him strong conflicts that he might overcome, and know that wisdom is mightier than all." [29]

101. It is related in the life of Blessed Henry Suso,[30] a Dominican friar, that in his ardent desire to possess Eternal Wisdom, he repeatedly offered to suffer every torment on condition of remaining in His good graces. One day he said to himself: "What! do you not know that lovers welcome unlimited suffering for the one who is the object of their love? Wakeful nights are sweet, fatigues are a pleasure, labors are repose to them, once they are assured that by all this they please and satisfy the person they love. If men do such things to please a mortal creature, do you not blush for shame to waver in your resolution to obtain Divine Wisdom? No, O Eternal Wisdom," he then exclaims, "I will never flinch from Thy love, were it necessary to go through the jungles and thickets of thorns to reach the place of Thy abode; were it necessary to undergo a thousand cruelties in soul and body, I will prize Thy friendship above everything else,

and Thou shalt be the absolute ruler of all my affections."

102. Some days later while traveling along a lonely road he fell among robbers. They beat him so mercilessly that the wretched state to which they had reduced him aroused even their pity. And now finding himself in this state without anyone to assist him, Henry Suso fell into a melancholy mood, forgot his resolution to bear manfully all afflictions, and began to weep and to wonder why God should thus have tried him. With this thought in mind he fell asleep. At daybreak he heard a voice which said reproachfully: "Behold our valiant soldier who skips over the mountains, climbs the rocks, storms the strongholds, who kills and cuts to pieces all his enemies when he is in a state of prosperity, but who has no courage, no arms, no feet, when misfortune has overtaken him. He is a lion in consolation, but a timid hart in tribulation. Eternal Wisdom does not entertain friendship with sluggards and cowards." Upon hearing these reproaches Blessed Henry Suso confessed to the fault he had committed by letting himself fall into an excess of melancholy; and he besought Wisdom to allow him to weep and to relieve his heart by letting his tears flow. "No, no," replied the voice, "the Blessed in heaven would entertain no esteem for you if you were to weep like a child or a woman; wipe away your tears and put on a happy face."

103. Thus we see that the cross is the portion as well as the reward of all those who seek after, or who already possess, Eternal Wisdom. But this loving Prince who numbers, weighs and measures all things, sends crosses to His friends only in proportion to their strength, and by the abundant unction of His own sweetness, He makes these crosses so delightful that they are borne with joy.

[1] Wisdom 8:22; [2] Wisdom 7:27; [3] Wisdom 10:16; [4] Wisdom 7.11; [5] Wisdom 7:7; [5a] Wisdom 8:11; [6] Wisdom 8:8; [7] Wisdom 10:10; [8] Wisdom 7:17; [9] Wisdom 7:21; [10] Wisdom 1:7; [11] Wisdom 10:21; [12] Ex. 4:10; [13] Jer. 1:9, 10; [14] Acts 2:11, Come Holy Ghost (Hymn); [15] I Thes. 2:13; [16] Hebrews 4:12; [17] Wisdom 7:15; [18] Luke 21:15; [19] 1 Cor. 2:7; [20] Wisdom 7:15, Matthew 12:34; [21] Acts 6:10; [22] 2 Cor. 7:4; [23] Wisdom 8:16; [24] Wisdom 7:12; [25] Wisdom 8:18; [26] Wisdom 8:7; [27] Wisdom 7:24; [28] Wisdom 3:3, 4, 5; [29] Wisdom 10:10-12; [30] For short sketch of his life and synopsis of his doctrine cf. Vie Spirituelle Vol. 24, pp. 32-53.

CHAPTER NINE

The Incarnation and the Life of Eternal Wisdom

104. When the Eternal Word, Eternal Wisdom, had decided in the grand council of the Blessed Trinity to become Man, for the restoration of fallen humanity, He probably made this known to Adam. As Scripture tells us, He promised the Patriarchs of the Old Law that He would become Man in order to redeem the world. Hence, during the ages which elapsed from the creation of the world to the Incarnation, all the just people of the Old Law begged for the coming of the Messiah, by their earnest prayers. They groaned, they wept, they cried out: "Let the clouds rain the Just One! Let the earth be opened and bud forth the Saviour." [1] "Wisdom Who didst proceed from the mouth of the Most High, come to deliver us." [2] But their cries, prayers and sacrifices had not the strength to draw Eternal Wisdom, the Son of God, from the bosom of His Father. They lifted up their arms toward Heaven, but these were not long enough to reach to the throne of the Most High. They continually offered sacrifices to God, even the sacrifice of their hearts, but these were not of sufficient merit to obtain this greatest of all graces.

105. At last, when the time appointed for the redemption of mankind had come, Eternal Wisdom built Himself a house — a worthy dwelling-place.[3] He created and formed the Immaculate Mary in the womb of St. Anne, which He did with even greater delight than He had taken in creating the universe. It is not possible to express, on the one hand, the ineffable communications of the Blessed Trinity to this most fair creature, and, on the other hand, the fidelity with which she corresponded with the graces of her Creator.

106. The precipitate current of the infinite goodness of God which had been violently checked by the sins of man, from the beginning of the world, now discharged itself impetuously and fully into the heart of Mary. To her, Eternal Wisdom gave all the graces which Adam and all his descendants would have received from His liberality, had they kept their original justice. The full plenitude of the graces of the Divinity poured itself into Mary, in so much as a mere creature is capable of receiving it. O Mary! Masterpiece of the Most High! Miracle of Eternal Wisdom! Prodigy of the Almighty! Abyss of grace! Only He Who created thee—and this I say with all the Saints— knows the height, the depth and the breadth of the graces He has conferred upon thee!

107. During her childhood and young maiden-

hood the Immaculate Mary grew so prodigiously in the grace and wisdom of God, and in perfect fidelity to His love, that not only the Angels but even God Himself was ravished with delight. Her humility, profound as an abyss, pleased Him; her complete purity drew Him to her; her lively faith and her frequent and loving prayers took Him by storm. Eternal Wisdom was lovingly conquered by her pursuit of love. St. Augustine exclaims, "O, how great was the love of Mary which conquered the Omnipotent!"

Wondrous act! When this Divine Wisdom wished to come down from the bosom of His Father into the womb of a virgin, to dwell there surrounded by the lilies of her purity, and to become hers by taking flesh in her, He sent the Archangel Gabriel to bring her His greetings, in order to betoken that she had won His heart, and that He wished to become Man in her, provided she gave her consent. The Archangel fulfilled his mission. He assured her that she would remain a virgin whilst becoming a mother, and thus obtained from her love the ineffable consent which the Blessed Trinity, all the Angels and the whole world had awaited for so many centuries. Profoundly humbling herself before the Creator, she said "Behold the handmaid of the Lord, be it done to me according to thy word." [4]

108. Notice that at the very moment Mary consented to become the Mother of God, several prodigies took place. The Holy Spirit began to form from the most pure blood of Mary's heart, a little Body which He fashioned most perfectly. God created the most perfect Soul that He ever created. Eternal Wisdom, the Son of God, truly united Himself in unity of person to that Body and Soul. Behold the great wonder of heaven and earth, the prodigious excess of the love of God! "The Word was made Flesh"; [5] Eternal Wisdom was incarnate; God was made Man without ceasing to be God. This God made Man is called Jesus Christ, which means Saviour.

Here is a summary of His divine life on earth.

109. 1. He wished to be born of a married woman—though she was indeed a virgin—that He might not be reproached as having been born of an adulterous union; and for other very important reasons given by the Holy Fathers. His conception was announced to the Blessed Virgin by the Angel Gabriel. He was made a child of Adam without inheriting his sin. The Church celebrates the day of His conception as the Feast of the Annunciation, March 25th.

110. 2. Nine months after His conception, the Saviour of the world was born in the town of Bethlehem, in a poor stable, with a manger for His cradle. An Angel brought the news of the Sav-

iour's birth to some shepherds who were keeping watch over their flocks in the fields; he invited them to go over to Bethlehem and adore their Saviour. At the same time they heard the celestial voices of Angels singing: "Glory to God in the highest, and peace on earth to men of good will." [6]

111. 3. Eight days after His birth He was circumcised according to the law of Moses, although He was not subject to the law, and He was given the name of Jesus, which was brought from heaven. Three Wise Men from the East came to adore Him. They were apprised of His birth by an extraordinary star which guided them throughout their long journey to Bethlehem. This is the Feast of the Epiphany, or the Manifestation of God, celebrated on January 6th.

112. 4. Forty days after His birth, He wished to offer Himself in the Temple that He might observe the ritual that the law of Moses prescribed for the firstborn. Some time after Jesus was presented in the Temple, the Angel told St. Joseph, Spouse of the Blessed Virgin, to take the Infant Jesus and His Mother and flee into Egypt, in order to escape the wrath of Herod. This he did. The length of time that Our Lord stayed in Egypt is not known, but by His presence He sanctified this whole country and made it worthy to be inhabited everywhere by the holy Hermits, as history proves. Eusebius tells us that at the entry of Jesus into Egypt, the devils

fled; and St. Athanasius adds that the idols toppled over.

113. 5. At the age of twelve years the Son of God, sitting among the Doctors in the Temple, taught with such wisdom that He astonished all His hearers. After this, the Gospel makes no mention of Him until He was baptized at the age of thirty. Then He retired into the desert, fasting from food and drink for forty days. He fought the devil and conquered him.

114. 6. After this He began to preach in Judea, to call the Apostles and to work all the miracles related in the Gospel. I need only record that Jesus, during the years of His public preaching, raised Lazarus from the dead; made a triumphant entrance into Jerusalem; celebrated the Pasch with His Disciples; washed the feet of His Apostles and instituted the Sacrament of the Holy Eucharist under the appearances of bread and wine.

115. 7. In the evening, a few hours after Christ had instituted the Holy Eucharist, He was apprehended by His enemies, with Judas the traitor leading them. The next day, notwithstanding this being the Feast of the Passover, He was condemned to death, scourged, crowned with thorns, and treated most ignominiously. That same day He was led to Calvary and nailed to a Cross between two thieves. In this manner the God of all inno-

cence wished to die the most shameful of all deaths, and to undergo the torments due to a robber named Barabbas whom the Jews had preferred to Him. The ancient Fathers hold that Jesus Christ was attached to the Cross by four nails, and that there was in the middle of the Cross a wooden bracket to support the body.*

116. 8. After three hours' agony the Saviour of the world died. Joseph of Arimathea had the courage to ask Pilate for the Body and laid It in a new sepulchre which he had built. We must not forget that nature expressed its sorrow at the death of its Maker by divers prodigies which took place at the moment of Christ's death. He rose again from the dead on the day we now celebrate as Easter Sunday.

---

* *Since Saint Louis De Montfort wrote this sentence, remarkable scientific discoveries in connection with the Holy Shroud of Turin have been made. These discoveries, fortified by additional investigation, seem to show that the Body of Our Redeemer was supported on the Cross by a large nail driven through each* **wrist** *and by another large nail driven through both feet. In Christ's time and in the days of the Prophets, the upper limbs were commonly believed to consist only of the arm and hand. Conversational or written reference would not be made to a "wrist." Hence, there is no discrepancy between the Holy Shroud evidence and Scriptural allusions to Christ's nailed "hand." For further information concerning these discoveries address* **The Holy Shroud Guild, Redemptorist Fathers, Esopus, New York.**

LOVE OF ETERNAL WISDOM

He appeared several times to His Mother and His disciples and, after forty days, He took His disciples to Mount Olivet. There, in their presence and by His own power, He ascended into heaven, to the right hand of His Father.

[1] Isaias 45:6 [2] Advent, Great Antiphons; [3] Prov. 9:1; [4] Luke 1:38; [5] John 1:14; [6] Luke 2:14.

CHAPTER TEN

*The captivating beauty and the ineffable
gentleness of Incarnate Wisdom
in His looks and words*

117. As Divine Wisdom became Man for the purpose of drawing the hearts of men to love and imitate Him, He was pleased to clothe Himself with all human gentleness and kindness in such an attractive and visible manner as to present no defect nor unsightliness.

118. If we consider Him in His origin, He is but goodness and meekness. He is a gift of the love of the Eternal Father and a manifestation of the love of the Holy Spirit. He was given through love and formed by love. "God so loved the world that He gave His only-begotten Son." [1] He is then all love, or rather He is the love of God the Father and of the Holy Spirit.

He was born of the sweetest, the most tender and the most beautiful of all mothers, the Immaculate Mary. If you would appreciate the gentleness of Jesus then consider first the gentleness of Mary, His Mother, whom He resembles by His pleasing character. Jesus is Mary's child; in Him there is no haughtiness, no harshness, no unpleasantness; and still less, infinitely less, in Him than in His Mother, because He is Eternal Wisdom; He is gentleness and beauty itself.

119. The Prophets who had, in advance, been shown this Incarnate Wisdom, called Him a lamb, "a meek lamb." [2] They foretold that because of His gentleness, "He would not break the bruised reed, nor quench the smoking flax"; [3] which means that because of His abundant mercy He will not allow the loss of a poor sinner, even though the sinner may be broken-down, blinded, depraved by sin, and having already as it were, one foot in hell— unless the sinner should compel Him to do so. St. John the Baptist lived in the desert, practicing austerities to obtain the knowledge and the love of Incarnate Wisdom; no sooner did he see Him coming than he pointed Him out to his disciples, exclaiming: "Behold the Lamb or God! Behold Him Who taketh away the sin of the world!" [4] He did not say, as it seems he should have said: Behold the Most High, behold the King of glory, behold the Almighty! But as he knew Him more thoroughly than any man who ever was or will be, he said: Behold the Lamb of God, behold Eternal Wisdom Who, to captivate our hearts and to take away our sins, has blended in His person all the meekness of God and of men, of heaven and of earth.

120. But what does the name of Jesus, which is the proper name of Incarnate Wisdom, signify, if not an ardent charity, an infinite love and attrac-

tive meekness? Jesus, Saviour, He Who saves man, and Whose characteristic is to love and save man.

> No voice can sing, no heart can frame,
> Nor can the memory find
> A sweeter sound than Thy blest Name,
> O Saviour of mankind.

Oh, how sweet is the name of Jesus to the ear and the heart of a soul seeking perfection! "A sweet honey in the mouth, a charming melody in the ear, a perfect exultation in the heart" (St. Bernard).

121. Jesus is gentle in His looks, in His words, in His actions.

The face of this loving Saviour is so serene and gentle that it charmed the eyes and the hearts of those who beheld Him. The shepherds who came to the stable to see Him were so spellbound by the serenity and beauty of His face that for several days they remained to gaze upon Him in rapture. The Kings, exalted as they were, had no sooner seen the loving features of this beautiful Child, than, laying aside their dignity, they fell on their knees by His crib. They must often have said to one another: "Friends, how good it is for us to be here! In our palaces we find no enjoyments to be compared with those we experience in this stable looking at this beloved Infant God."

Tradition tells us that when Jesus was still very young, afflicted people and children in the vicinity went to see Him to find comfort and joy. They said to one another: "Let us go to see little Jesus, the beautiful Child of Mary." St. Chrysostom writes: "The beauty and majesty of His face were at once so sweet and so worthy of respect, that those who knew Him could not but love Him; and kings from afar, hearing of His beauty, wanted to have His painting." It is even said that Our Lord by special favor sent the image of His face to King Abogare. Some writers tell us that the Roman soldiers and Jews covered His face, during the scourging, to strike and buffet Him more freely, because there was in His eyes and face such a sweet and ravishing display of beauty as would have disarmed the most cruel of men.

122. Jesus is also gentle in His words. When on earth, He conquered all by the meekness of His words. Never was He heard to cry out loudly or to argue heatedly. This was foretold by the Prophets.[5] Those who listened to Him with good will, were charmed by the words of life which fell from His lips. They said: "Never did man speak like this man";[6] and those who hated Him were surprised upon hearing His eloquence and wisdom. Never did a man speak with such meekness and unction. Whence did He have so much wisdom in His speech?[7] Multitudes of poor people left their homes

and families to go and hear Him, even in the desert. They spent many days without eating and drinking, but they were filled by the meekness of His words. This meekness of His words was the bait which drew the Apostles after Him; it was the balm which healed the most incurable, and which comforted the most afflicted. To the disconsolate Mary Magdalen He spoke but one word, "Mary," and she was overwhelmed with joy and happiness.

[1] John 3:16;   [2] Jer. 11:19;   [3] Isaias 42:3;   [4] John 1:29;   [5] Isaias 42:2;   Matthew 12:19;   [6] John 7:46;   [7] Matthew 13:54.

CHAPTER ELEVEN

*The gentleness of Incarnate Wisdom in
His actions*

123. Finally, Jesus is gentle in His actions. This gentleness may be observed throughout the whole course of His life. "He has done all His actions well." [1] Which means that all that Jesus Christ did was done with such exactitude, wisdom, holiness and meekness that nothing faulty or wanting can be found in what He did. Let us consider how gently this loving Incarnate Wisdom acted in all His ways.

124. The poor and the little children followed Him everywhere as one of their own. The simplicity, kindliness, courtesy, charity they noticed in this dear Saviour caused them to throng about Him. One day when He was preaching, the children who were habitually with their mothers, pressed close to Him. The Apostles who were nearest to Our Lord rebuked the children. Upon seeing this, Jesus said to His Apostles: "Suffer little children to come unto Me." [2]

When they came near Him He embraced and blessed them. O, what sweetness and kindness! The poor, seeing Him dressed like the poor, simple in His manners, without ostentation or haughtiness, enjoyed His company. They stood by Him against the rich and the proud when these calumniated and persecuted Him. He, in His turn, praised and blessed them upon every occasion.

125. But who will explain to us the gentleness of Jesus in His dealings with poor sinners? His gentleness with Mary Magdalen, the public sinner? His gracious condescension in converting the Samaritan woman? His mercy in pardoning the adulterous woman? His charity when He sat down to eat with public sinners in order to win them? Did not His enemies take His great kindness as a pretext to persecute Him, saying that He countenanced the transgression of the law of Moses, and tauntingly called Him the friend of sinners and of publicans? How kindly and humbly did He not try to win over the heart of Judas who intended to betray Him, when He washed his feet and called him friend! And how charitably did He ask the pardon of God, His Father, for His executioners, pleading their ignorance as an excuse!

126. Oh, how beautiful, how meek, how charitable is Jesus, Incarnate Wisdom! Beautiful in eternity, for "He is the brightness of His Father, the unspotted mirror and the image of His goodness." [3] He is more beautiful than the sun, brighter than light itself! Beautiful in time, because the Holy Ghost formed Him pure without sin, fair without stain. Beautiful because, during His life, He charmed the eyes and the hearts of men, and because He is now the glory of Angels. How loving and gentle He is

with all of us, poor sinners whom He came to seek visibly in this world, and whom He now seeks invisibly every day!

127. Do you think that Jesus, now that He is triumphant and glorious, is any the less loving and condescending. On the contrary, His glory perfects, as it were, His mercy. He wishes to forgive rather than to be exalted, and to display the riches of His mercy rather than those of His glory.

128. Read what is related of Him and you will see that when this Incarnate and glorious Wisdom appeared to His friends, He appeared to them, not in thunder and lightning, but meekly and gently; not assuming the majesty of a king or of the Lord of Hosts, but with the tenderness of a spouse, the kindness of a friend. Sometimes, He has appeared in the Holy Eucharist, but I cannot remember having read that He ever did so, except under the form of a meek and beautiful child.

129. Not long ago, an unfortunate man, raging mad because he had lost all his money by gambling, drew his sword against heaven, blaming Our Lord for the loss of his money. Astonishing result! Instead of thunderbolts and fiery darts falling upon him, behold, a little piece of paper comes fluttering about above his head! In amazement the man catches it, opens it, and reads: "Have mercy on me, O God!" [4] The sword falls from his hand; he is

moved to the depths of his heart, falls on his knees and begs for mercy.

130. St. Denis the Areopagite relates that a certain Bishop, Carpus by name, after much labor, converted a pagan. Upon hearing afterward that a fellow pagan had made this convert abjure the faith, Carpus earnestly entreated God, during a whole night, to wreak vengeance for the injury done to His Majesty by punishing the guilty ones. Suddenly, when at the height of fervor in his prayer, Carpus saw the earth open, and on the brink of hell he perceived the apostate and the pagan whom the demons were trying to drag down into the abyss. And now lifting up his eyes, he saw heaven open and Jesus Christ accompanied by a multitude of Angels, coming to him and saying: "Carpus, you ask Me to take vengeance. But you do not know Me. Do you realize what you ask, and the price which I have paid for sinners? Why do you want Me to cast them away? I love them so, that if it were necessary, I would be ready to die again for each one of them." Then Our Lord, coming near to Carpus and showing His naked shoulders, said: "Carpus, if you want to take vengeance, strike Me rather than these poor sinners."

131. Knowing this, shall we not love this Eternal Wisdom Who has loved and still loves us more than His own life? Whose beauty and meekness surpass all that is lovely and gentle in heaven and on earth?

132. We read in the life of Blessed Henry Suso

how Eternal Wisdom, Whom he had so ardently desired, appeared to him one day in human form, surrounded by a light transparent cloud, and seated upon a throne of ivory. Radiating from His eyes and face was a brightness like the rays of the sun at midday. His crown represented eternity; His robes, blessedness; His word, meekness; and His embrace brought the fullness of bliss to all the Blessed. Henry contemplated Him in this array. What surprised him most was to see Eternal Wisdom now under the aspect of a young maiden, the prodigy of heavenly and earthly beauty; now under the form of a young man whose countenance reflected all the beauties to be found on earth. At other times he perceived Him far away, and then coming near. Now He looked full of majesty; now condescending, gentle, meek, and tender to all who approached Him. At this moment, Eternal Wisdom turned to Henry and said to him, with an inviting smile: "My son, give Me thy heart." [5] At once, Henry threw himself at His feet, and offered Him irrevocably his heart.

After the example of this holy man let us also offer forever to Eternal Wisdom the gift of our heart. He asks for nothing more.

[1] Mark 7:37;   [2] Mark 10:14;   [3] Wisdom 7:26;
[4] Ps. 50:1;   [5] Prov. 23:26.

Chapter Twelve

The solemn Utterances of Incarnate Wisdom, which we must believe and practice to be saved

Translator's Note

This chapter should not be looked upon as dry quotations from the Gospels, chosen at random. It forms the central part of the book. To realize the importance which St. Louis de Montfort attaches to this chapter it suffices to read his conclusion in this regard. (No. 153.)

To come to the perfect possession of Divine Wisdom we must accept and follow His teaching. We must begin to renouncing ourselves and keeping the great Commandment of loving God and our neighbor. (No. 133.) We must renounce the flesh, the world and its temporal goods. (No. 134.) Above all we must renounce our self-will. (No. 135.) To do this we must humbly pray, (No. 136) we must do penance, (Nos. 137, 138) and suffer persecution. (No. 139.) For all this we need the help of Divine Wisdom Who invites us to go to Him. (No. 140.) With His help we need not fear (No. 141) provided we be clean of heart. (No. 143.) To succeed we must persevere, not look back, (No. 144), and we must walk in the light and act according to the

teachings of Divine Wisdom, (Nos. 145, 146);
we must be vigilant and avoid the maxims of the
false prophets, (No. 147); we must not fear what
may be done to our body and reputation, (No. 148)
but only be solicitous about the kingdom of God
(No. 149) which we can only enter by the narrow
gate. (No. 150.) Therefore we must keep in mind
the eight Beatitudes (No. 151) and we must be
thankful to God for having taught us these heavenly
truths. (No. 152.)

Self Denial

133. "If any man will come after Me, let him
deny himself, and take up his cross daily and follow
Me.[1] If any man love Me, he will keep My word,
and My Father will love him and we will come to
him.[2] If therefore thou offer thy gift at the altar,
and there thou remember that thy brother hath anything against thee; leave there thy offering before
the altar, and go first to be reconciled to thy
brother." [3]

134. "If any man come to Me, and hate not his
father and mother and wife and children and brethren and sisters, yea, and his own life also, he cannot
be My disciple.[4] Every one that hath left house, or
brethren, or sisters, or father or mother or wife or
children or lands for My name's sake, shall receive
a hundredfold, and shall possess life everlasting.[5]

If thou wilt be perfect, go sell what thou hast, and give to the poor, and thou shalt have treasure in heaven." [6]

135. "Not every one that shall say to Me, Lord, Lord, shall enter into the kingdom of heaven, but he that doth the will of My Father, Who is in heaven, he shall enter into the kingdom of heaven.[7] Every one therefore that heareth My words, and doth them, shall be likened to a wise man that built his house upon a rock.[8] Amen, I say to you, unless you be converted, and become as little children, you shall not enter into the kingdom of heaven.[9] Learn from Me because I am meek and humble of heart, and you shall find rest to your souls." [10]

Prayer

136. "When ye pray, you shall not be as the hypocrites that love to stand and pray in the synagogues that they may be seen by men.[11] When you are praying, speak not much as the heathens, for your Father knoweth what is needful for you, before you ask Him.[12] When you shall stand to pray, forgive, if you have aught against any man, that your Father who is in heaven, may forgive you your sins.[13] All things whatever you ask when ye pray, believe that you shall receive, and they shall come to you." [14]

Penance

137. "When you fast be not as the hypocrites, sad. For they disfigure their faces, that they may appear unto man to fast. Amen I say to you they have received their reward." [15]

138. "There shall be joy in heaven upon one sinner that doth penance, more than upon the ninety-n.ne just who need not penance.[16] I come not to call the just, but sinners to penance." [17]

139. "Blessed are they that suffer persecution for justice' sake; for theirs is the kingdom of heaven.[18] Blessed are ye when they shall hate you, and when they shall separate you, and shall reproach you and cast you out for the Son of man's sake. Be glad in that day and rejoice for behold your reward is great in heaven.[19] If the world hate you, know ye that it hath hated Me before you. If you had been of the world, the world would love its own; but because I have chosen you out of the world, therefore the world hateth you." [20]

God's Help

140. "Come to Me all you that labor and are burdened, and I will refresh you.[21] I am the living bread which came down from heaven. If any man eat of this bread, he shall live for ever, and the bread that I will give is My flesh.[22] My flesh is meat indeed and My blood is drink indeed. He that eateth My

flesh, and drinketh My blood, abideth in Me and I in him." [23]

141. "You shall be hated by all men for My name's sake. But a hair of your head shall not perish." [24]

142. "No man can serve two masters. For either he will hate the one and love the other, or he will sustain the one and despise the other." [25]

Clean of Heart

143. "From the heart come forth evil thoughts that defile a man; but to eat with unwashed hands doth not defile a man.[26] A good man out of a good treasure bringeth forth good things, and an evil man out of an evil treasure bringeth forth evil things." [27]

144. "No man putting his hand to the plough, and looking back, is fit for the kingdom of God.[28] Yea, the very hairs of your head are all numbered. Fear not therefore, you are of more value than many sparrows.[29] God sent not His Son into the world, to judge the world, but that the world may be saved by Him." [30]

Follow His Teachings

145. "Every one that doth evil hateth the light, and cometh not to the light, that his works may not be reproved.[31] God is a spirit, and they that adore

Him, must adore Him in spirit and in truth.[32] It is the spirit that quickeneth, the flesh profiteth nothing. The words that I have spoken to you, are spirit and life.[33] Whosoever committeth sin, is the servant of sin; now the servant abideth not in the house for ever.[34] He that is faithful in that which is least, is faithful also in that which is greater; and he that is unjust in that which is little, is unjust also in that which is greater.[35] It is easier for heaven and earth to pass than one tittle of the law to fall.[36] So let your light shine before men that they may see your good works and glorify your Father who is in heaven." [37]

146. "Unless your justice abound more than that of the scribes and Pharisees, you shall not enter into the kingdom of heaven.[38] If thy right eye scandalize thee, pluck it out and cast it from thee, for it is expedient for thee that one of thy members should perish, rather than that thy whole body be cast into hell.[39] The kingdom of heaven suffereth violence, and the violent bear it away.[40] Lay not up to yourselves treasures on earth, where the rust and moth consume, and where thieves break through and steal. But lay up to yourselves treasures in heaven, where neither the rust nor moth consume, and where thieves do not break through nor steal.[41] Judge not that you may not be judged; for with what judgment you judge, you shall be judged." [42]

False Prophets

147. "Beware of false prophets who come to you in the clothing of sheep, but inwardly they are ravening wolves. By their fruits you shall know them.[43] See that you despise not one of these little ones, for I say to you that their Angels in heaven always see the face of My Father who is in heaven.[44] Watch ye therefore because you know not the day nor the hour" (when the Lord will come).[45]

148. "Be not afraid of them that kill the body, and after that have no more they can do; but fear Him who after He hath killed, hath power to cast into hell.[46] Be not solicitous for your life what you shall eat, nor for your body what you shall put on. Your Father knoweth that you have need of these things.[47] There is not anything secret that shall not be made manifest, nor hidden that shall not be known." [48]

Narrow Gate

149. "Whosoever will be the greater among you, let him be your minister; and he that will be the first among you, shall be your servant.[49] How hardly shall they that have riches enter into the kingdom of God.[50] It is easier for a camel to pass through the eye of a needle, than for a rich man to enter into the kingdom or God.[51] I say to you, love your

enemies; do good to them that hate you, and pray for them that persecute and calumniate you.[52] Woe to you that are rich; for you have your consolation." [53]

150. "Enter ye in at the narrow gate, for wide is the gate and broad is the way that leadeth to destruction, and many there are who go in there. How narrow is the gate, and strait is the way that leadeth to life, and few there are that find it.[54] The last shall be first and the first last for many are called but few are chosen.[55] It is a more blessed thing to give rather than to receive.[56] If one strike thee on the right cheek, turn to him also the other; and if a man will contend with thee in judgment, and take away thy coat let go thy cloak also to him.[57] We ought always to pray, and not to faint.[58] Watch ye and pray that ye enter not into temptation.[59] Give alms; and behold, all things are clean unto you.[60] Every one that exalteth himself shall be humbled, and he that humbleth himself shall be exalted.[61] If thy hand or thy foot scandalize thee, cut it off and cast it from thee. It is better for thee to go into life maimed, or lame, than having two hands or two feet, to be cast into everlasting fire. And if thy eye scandalize thee, pluck it out and cast it from thee. It is better for thee having one eye to enter into life, than having two eyes to be cast into hell fire." [62]

Eight Beatitudes

151. "Blessed are the poor in spirit; for theirs is the kingdom of heaven.

Blessed are the meek; for they shall possess the land.

Blessed are they that mourn; for they shall be comforted.

Blessed are they that hunger and thirst after justice; for they shall have their fill.

Blessed are the merciful; for they shall obtain mercy.

Blessed are the clean of heart; for they shall see God.

Blessed are the peacemakers; for they shall be called the children of God.

Blessed are they that suffer persecution for justice' sake; for theirs is the kingdom of heaven." [63]

152. "I confess to Thee, O Father, Lord of heaven and earth, because Thou hast hid these things from the wise and prudent, and hast revealed them to little ones. Yea, Father; for so hath it seemed good in Thy sight." [64]

153. Such is the summary of the great and important truths which Eternal Wisdom came to teach us on earth—after having first practiced them Him-

self—in order to cure us from the blindness and the aberrations into which our sins had led us.

Blessed are they who understand eternal truths.

More blessed are they who believe them.

But most blessed are they who believe them, who practice them, and who teach them to others, for like stars they will shine in heaven for all eternity.

[1] Luke 9:23;   [2] John 14:23;   [3] Matt. 5:23, 24;   [4] Luke 14:26;   [5] Matt. 19:29;   [6] Matt. 19:21;   [7] Matt. 7:21;   [8] Matt. 7:24;   [9] Matt. 18:3;   [10] Matt. 11:29;   [11] Matt. 6:5;   [12] Matt. 6:7, 8;   [13] Mark 11:25;   [14] Mark 11:24;   [15] Matt. 6:16;   [16] Luke 15:7;   [17] Luke 5:32;   [18] Matt. 5:10;   [19] Luke 6:22, 23;   [20] John 15:18, 19;   [21] Matt. 11:28;   [22] John 6:51, 52;   [23] John 6:56, 57;   [24] Luke 21:17, 18;   [25] Matt. 6:24;   [26] Matt. 15:19, 20;   [27] Matt. 12:35;   [28] Luke 9:62;   [29] Luke 12:7;   [30] John 3:17;   [31] John 3:20;   [32] John 4:24;   [33] John 6:64;   [34] John 8:34, 35;   [35] Luke 16:10;   [36] Luke 16:17;;   [37] Matt. 5:16;   [38] Matt. 5:20;   [39] Matt. 5:29;   [40] Matt. 11:12;   [41] Matt. 6:19, 20;   [42] Matt. 7:1, 2;   [43] Matt. 7:15;   [44] Matt. 18:10;   [45] Matt. 25:13;   [46] Luke 12:4, 5;   [47] Luke 12:22, 30;   [48] Luke 8:17;   [49] Matt. 20:26, 27;   [50] Mark 10:23;   [51] Luke 18:25;   [52] Matt. 5:44;   [53] Luke 6:24;   [54] Matt. 7:13, 14;   [55] Matt. 20:16;   [56] Act. 20:35;   [57] Matt. 5:39, 40;   [58] Luke 18:1;   [59] Matt. 26:41;   [60] Luke 11:41;   [61] Luke 14:11;   [62] Matt. 18:8, 9;   [63] Matt. 5:3 to 10;   [64] Matt. 11:25, 26.

CHAPTER THIRTEEN

A summary of the unutterable Sorrows which Incarnate Wisdom suffered for love of us

154. Among all the motives which urge us to love Jesus Christ, Incarnate Wisdom, the strongest is, in my opinion, the sorrows which He endured to show us His love. "There is," says St. Bernard, "one motive which excels them all, which spurs me on more affectionately, and urges me to love Jesus Christ, and it is, my good Jesus, the bitter chalice which Thou didst drink for us, and the works of the Redemption which make Thee so dear to our hearts, for this supreme blessing and incomparable token of Thy love readily gains our love. This motive draws us more gently; it claims us more justly; it impels us more stringently; it moves us more forcibly." In these few words St. Bernard shows us how much our dear Saviour has labored and suffered to achieve the work of our Redemption. O, the pangs and the agony He has endured!

155. But it is the circumstances which accompanied His sufferings that will make us realize more clearly the infinite love of Eternal Wisdom for us.

The first of these is the *excellence of His Person*, which being infinite gives infinite value to all the sufferings of His Passion. Had God sent a Seraphim, or an angel of the lowest order, to make himself man and to die for us, it would have been a wonderful thing worthy of our eternal gratitude. Instead, the Creator of heaven and earth, the only Son of God, Eternal Wisdom Himself, came to offer His life! In comparison with this the lives of all the angels, of all mankind and of all living creatures are infinitely less than is the life of a gnat compared with the lives of all the kings of this earth. What excess of love are we shown in this mystery, and what ought to be our admiration and our gratitude!

156. The second circumstance is the *condition of the people* for whom He suffers. They are mere men, abject creatures; they are His enemies from whom He has nothing to fear, nor anything to expect. Sometimes, we hear of friends dying for their friends, but shall we ever hear of anyone but the Son of God dying for His enemies? "But God commendeth His charity toward us, because when as yet we were sinners (and consequently His enemies), Christ died for us." [1]

157. The third circumstance is *the number, the grievousness and the duration of His sufferings*. The number of His sufferings was so great that He is called *vir dolorum*; "a Man of all sorrows in Whom there is no soundness from the sole of the foot unto the top of the head." [2] This dear Friend of our souls suffered in all things exteriorly and interiorly, in His body and in His soul.

158. He suffered *in what He possessed;* for, not to mention the poverty of His birth, of His flight

into Egypt and of His entire life, He was, during His Passion, stripped by the soldiers who "parted His garments amongst them," [3] and fixed Him naked to the gibbet, not leaving Him so much as a rag to cover His body.

159. He suffered in *His honor and reputation*, for He was overwhelmed with reproaches, and called a blasphemer, a seducer, a wine drinker, a glutton and one having a devil.

In His wisdom, because they treated Him as an ignorant man, as an imposter, as a fool, as a madman.

In His power, for they held Him as a sorcerer and magician who worked false miracles by a compact with the devil.

160. *In His disciples*, one of whom sold and betrayed Him, the first of whom denied Him, the rest of whom abandoned Him.

He suffered from *people of all kinds*: that is, from kings, governors, judges, courtiers, soldiers, pontiffs, priests, clerical and lay people, from Jews and Gentiles, from men and women, and in fact from everybody. Even His Blessed Mother added dreadfully to His affliction when, as He was dying, He saw her standing at the foot of the cross, immersed in an ocean of sadness.

161. Our dear Saviour has also suffered *in all the members of His body*. His head was crowned with thorns; hairs were torn from His head and beard;

His cheeks were buffeted, His face was spit upon, His neck and His arms were bound with cords, His shoulders were bent and bruised by the weight of the Cross. His hands and feet were pierced by nails, His side and His heart opened by a lance, His whole body pitilessly lacerated by more than 5,000 strokes of the scourge, so that His almost fleshless bones became visible to the eye. His five senses were also immersed in this sea of suffering: sight, when He beheld the mocking faces of His enemies and the tears of grief of His friends; hearing, when He heard the insults, the false testimonies, the calumnies and the horrible blasphemies which accursed lips uttered against Him; smell, when tortured by the stench of the filth which was hurled in His face; taste, by the feverish thirst which his executioners increased by giving Him gall and vinegar to drink; touch, by the excruciating pains caused by the lashes, the thorns and the nails.

162. *His most holy soul* was grievously tormented because of the sins of all men. These sins were so many outrages against His Father Whom He infinitely loved. They were the cause of the damnation of so many souls that would be lost despite His Passion and Death. He was also tormented because He had compassion not only upon all men in general, but upon every one in particular, as He knew them all individually.

All these torments were much increased by *their*

duration, for they lasted from the first instant of His Incarnation to the moment of His death. In the infinite light of His wisdom, all the sufferings He was to endure were always and distinctly present in His mind.

To all these torments we must add the most cruel and more appalling of them all: *His abandonment upon the Cross* which caused Him to cry out, "My God, My God, why hast Thou forsaken Me?" [4]

163. From all this, then, we must conclude with St. Thomas and the Holy Fathers that our good Jesus has suffered more than all the martyrs together, including those who have been and those who will be until the end of the world. Now, if the least suffering of the Son of God is more precious and more capable of moving our hearts than all the sufferings of all the angels and all men had they died and reduced themselves to nothing for us, how deep then must be our grief and also our love and gratitude to Him, because He has suffered for us of His own free will and with the utmost love all that one can suffer! "Having joy set before Him, He endured the cross." [5] This, according to the Holy Fathers, means that when Jesus Christ, Eternal Wisdom, could have remained in His heavenly glory, infinitely distant from our miseries, He preferred, on our account, to come down upon earth, to make Himself Man and to be crucified. When He had become Man, He could have enjoyed in His body the same

joy, the same immortality, the same beatitude which He now enjoys, but He did not wish this in order that He might be able to suffer.

164. Rupert (Abbot Bishop of Salzburg, famous for his learning and piety; died in 718) adds that, at the Incarnation, the Eternal Father proposed to His Son to save the world either by joy or by affliction, by honors or by contempt, by riches or by poverty, by life or by death. Hence, He could have redeemed man and taken us to heaven with Him by joys, pleasures, honors, and riches, had He wished to do so, whilst remaining Himself glorious and triumphant. He chose rather to endure the Cross and sufferings in order to give to God, His Father, greater glory, and to man a token of greater love.

165. Nay, more, He loved us so that instead of abridging His sorrows, He prolonged them, wishing to suffer a thousand times more. This is the reason why, when hanging on the Cross, and already overwhelmed with reproaches and sunk in grief, He, as if not suffering enough, cried out: "I thirst." [6] What does He thirst after? St. Lawrence Justinian answers: "His thirst was caused by the ardor of His love, by the source and the abundance of His charity. He was athirst for us, to give Himself to us and suffer for us."

166. Knowing all this, let us exclaim with St. Francis of Paula: "O Love, O God of Love!, how excessive is the love which Thou hast shown to us

in suffering and dying." Or with St. Mary Magdalen de Pazzi while kissing the crucifix: "O Love, O Love, how little art Thou known!" Or else with St. Francis of Assisi trailing through the mud of the streets: "O, Jesus, my crucified Love, is not known; Jesus, my Love, is not loved!" Each day Holy Mother Church repeats St. John's words: "The world does not know Jesus Christ." [7] And, to speak rightly, it is morally impossible to know what Our Lord has endured for us, and yet, like the world, not to love Him ardently.

[1] Rom. 5:8, 9;   [2] Isaias 53:3;   [3] Ps. 21:19;
[4] Matt. 27:46;   [5] Heb. 12:2;   [6] John 19:28;
[7] John 1:10.

CHAPTER FOURTEEN

*The Triumph of Eternal Wisdom in and through
the cross **

167. The Cross is, to my belief, the greatest
"secret of the King"; [1] the greatest mystery of
Eternal Wisdom.

O how distant and how different are the thoughts
and the ways of Eternal Wisdom from those of man,
even the most wise! This great God wishes to redeem the world, to cast out and shackle the demons,
to close hell and to open heaven to man, and to
render infinite glory to His Eternal Father. Such
is His purpose, His arduous task, His great enter-
prise. What means will be chosen by the Divine
Wisdom Who by His knowledge "reaches from end
to end mightily, and orders all things sweetly"? [2]
His arm is almighty. In a thrice He can destroy
all that is opposed to Him. He can create whatever
He wills. By one word of His mouth He can anni-
hilate and create. What do I say? He has but to
will to do all things.

168. But His love gives the law to His power.
He wishes to become incarnate in order to convince
man of His friendship. He wishes to come down
upon earth in order to make man ascend into heaven.

---

* This is the most beautiful and most impressive Chapter of this book. Someone has called it Montfort's triumph
as well as the triumph of Christ.

So be it. It would appear that this Incarnate Wisdom will come glorious and triumphant, accompanied by millions and millions of Angels, or at least by millions of chosen men. With these armies, He, glittering with majesty, not poor, not dishonorable, not low, not weak, will crush all His enemies and win the hearts of men by His charm, His favors, His honors and riches. Nothing less than all that. But, O wonder! He perceives a thing which is a scandal and a stumbling block to the Jews, an object of foolishness to the Gentiles.[3] He sees a piece of vile and contemptible wood which is being used to humiliate and torture the most wicked and most unfortunate of men; it is called a gibbet, a gallows, a Cross. He looks upon this Cross. He takes delight in it. He loves it and chooses it before all that is great and resplendent in heaven and on earth. He chooses it to be the instrument of His conquests, the adornment of His majesty, the riches and delight of His empire, the friend and spouse of His heart. "O the depth of the wisdom and of the knowledge of God!"[4] How amazing His choice! How deep and incomprehensible His way of acting and judging! But how ineffable His love of the Cross!

169. The Incarnate Wisdom loved the Cross from His infancy.[5] At His coming into the world He received it from the hands of His Eternal Father in the womb of His Mother. He placed it "in the

midst of His heart," [6] there to reign. Amplifying the words of the Psalmist He must have cried: "My God and My Father, I chose this Cross when I was in Thy bosom. I choose it now in the womb of My Mother. I love it with all My strength and I place it in the midst of My heart to be My spouse and My Mistress."

170. During His life He eagerly sought after the Cross. If, like a thirsting hart, He hastened from hamlet to hamlet, from town to town; if with giant strides He moved on to Calvary; if He spoke so frequently of His sufferings and death to His Apostles and disciples, and even to His Prophets during the Transfiguration; if often He exclaimed: "with desire I have desired," [7] it was because all His journeying, all His eagerness, all His pursuits, all His desires were directed toward the Cross, and, because to die in its embrace was for Him the very height of glory and success.

With ineffable delight He espoused the Cross in His Incarnation. With unutterable joy He looked for it and bore it during His whole life, which was but one continuous Cross; and after having made repeated efforts to embrace it and to die upon it on Calvary, He exclaimed: "I have a baptism wherewith I am to be baptized: and how am I straitened until it be accomplished?" [8]

171. At last His wishes were fully satisfied. Loaded with infamy He was attached to the Cross,

fixed to it, and joyfully died in the embrace of His dear friend as upon a couch of honor and triumph.

172. Do not think that, to be more triumphant, He relinquished or rejected the Cross after His death. Far from it. He united Himself so closely to it and became, as it were, so incorporated with it, that no angel or man, no creature in heaven or on earth can separate Him from it. Their bond is indissoluble; their union is eternal. NEVER THE CROSS WITHOUT JESUS; NOR JESUS WITHOUT THE CROSS.

By His death the ignominies of the Cross were made so glorious, its poverty and bareness so opulent, its pains so sweet, its hardness so attractive, that it became as it were deified and an object of adoration for angels and men. Jesus now demands that, with Him, all His subjects adore it. It is not His wish that a worship even of a relative adoration should be given to any other creatures however high they be, such as His most holy Mother, but this worship is due and rendered only to His dear Cross. *

On the day of the last judgment He will bring to an end all the relics of the Saints, even the most worthy of respect, but as for those of His Cross He will command the chief Seraphim and Cherubim to

* It should be carefully noted that Montfort speaks here of the worship of *adoration* which the Church renders to no other creature but the True Cross on which Christ died.

gather up throughout the whole world all the particles of the true Cross, and they will be so well reunited by His loving omnipotence that they will form but one Cross, the very Cross upon which He died. He will have His Cross borne in triumph by the angels who will sing its joyful praises. His Cross will go before Him placed upon the most brilliant cloud that ever appeared. He will judge the world with His Cross and by it. What will be the joy of the friends of the Cross on beholding it. What will be the despair of its enemies, who not being able to bear the brilliant sight of this Cross will cry out to the mountains to fall upon them, and to the depths of hell to swallow them up!

173. Whilst waiting for the great and triumphant day of the last judgment, Eternal Wisdom wants the Cross to be the sign, the mark and the weapon of His elect. He now receives no child that is not marked with its character. He admits no disciple who does not bear its sign on his forehead without being ashamed of it, on his heart without despising it, and on his shoulders without dragging it or shaking it off. He exclaims: "If any man will come after Me, let him deny himself, and take up his cross and follow Me." [9] He enlists no soldier who does not take the Cross as the weapon to defend himself against all his enemies, to attack, to conquer, and to crush them. He told His disciples to "have confidence" [10] in Him. We can imagine

Him saying to us: "My soldiers, I am your leader. I have conquered My enemies by the Cross. You will also conquer by this sign."

174. He has laid up so many great treasures of grace, of life and of joy in the Cross that He makes them known only to His great favorites. He often discloses to His friends all other secrets, as He did to the Apostles: "all things I have made known to you." [11] But the secrets of the Cross He reveals only to those who make themselves worthy of them by their perfect fidelity and their great labors. O, how humble one must be, how little, how mortified, how interior, how despised by the world, to come to know the mystery of the Cross, which even today is an object of scandal and folly not only to the Jews and pagans, to the Turks and heretics, to the worldly-wise and bad Catholics, but even to the so-called devout, even the very devout people. Yes, the Cross remains an object of scandal and folly, of contempt and fear, although not in theory, for the Cross is spoken of more than ever, and much is written about its beauty and its excellence. In practice, however, people fear, complain, excuse themselves and shrink as soon as there is a question of suffering.

"My Father," said the Incarnate Wisdom, when beholding in a rapture of joy the beauties of the Cross, "I confess to Thee, because Thou hast hidden these things from the wise and prudent of this world, and hast revealed them to little ones." [12]

175. If the knowledge of the mystery of the Cross is such a very special grace, what then must be the enjoyment of its actual possession? This is a gift which Eternal Wisdom bestows only on His best friends and only after they have implored it with many prayers and ardent desires. However excellent be the gift of faith by which we please God and come to Him, and by which we conquer our enemies, and without which we shall be lost, yet the knowledge of the Cross is a greater gift.

"It is a greater happiness for St. Peter," writes St. John Chrysostom, "to be imprisoned for Jesus Christ than to be with Him in His glory on Mount Thabor; it is greater glory for him to wear his prisoner's chains than to bear in his hands the keys to Paradise." St. Paul reckons it a greater glory to be in chains for his Saviour than to be taken up to the third heaven. God bestowed a greater favor on the Apostles and Martyrs when He gave them His Cross to carry in their humiliations, their privations, their cruel torments, than when He conferred upon them the gift of miracles and the graces necessary for the conversion of souls. All those to whom Eternal Wisdom communicated Himself were desirous of the Cross. They sought after it. They embraced it. Whenever they had an occasion to suffer, they exclaimed from the bottom of their hearts, like St.

Andrew: "O good cross for which I have wished so long." [13]

176. The Cross is good and precious for many reasons:

1. Because it makes us resemble Jesus Christ.

2. Because it makes us worthy children of the Eternal Father; worthy members of Jesus Christ; worthy temples of the Holy Spirit: "God the Father . . . scourgeth every son He receives." [14] Jesus Christ receives as His follower only him who carries his cross. The Holy Spirit cuts and polishes all the living stones of the heavenly Jerusalem; that is, the souls seeking perfection. These are revealed truths.

3. The Cross is good because it enlightens the mind and affords more knowledge than all the books in the whole world. "He that has not been tried, what does he know?" [15]

4. Because when well borne the Cross is the cause, the nourishment and the proof of love. The Cross inflames the heart with the fire of divine love by detaching it from creatures; it keeps this love alive and increases it. As wood is the fuel of fire, so is the Cross the fuel of love. The Cross is the surest proof that we love God. The Cross was the proof God gave of His love for us, and it is also the proof He requires of us to show our love for Him.

5. The Cross is good because it is an abundant

source of all kinds of delight and consolation. It brings joy, peace and grace to the soul.

6. The Cross is good because "it worketh" for the one who carries it, "an eternal weight of glory." [16]

177. If we knew the value of the Cross, we would, like St. Peter Alcantara, pray unceasingly to acquire this select portion of paradise. We would say like St. Theresa: "either to suffer or to die"; or like St. Mary Magdalene de Pazzi: "not to die, but to suffer." We would, like St. John of the Cross, ask only for "the grace to suffer and to be despised for thee." "In heaven nothing among the things of this world is valued but the Cross," the same St. John of the Cross declared to a saintly person during a vision, after his death. And Our Lord said one day to one of His servants: "I have crosses of such great price that My Mother, all powerful though she be, can obtain nothing more precious from Me for her faithful servants."

178. You, who are wise and honest by worldly standards, do not understand this mysterious language. You are too fond of sensual pleasures; you seek too much your own comfort; you love too much the things of this life; you fear too much to be held up to scorn and to be humiliated; in a word, you are too hostile to the Cross of Jesus. In general, indeed, you esteem and praise the Cross, but not your personal crosses. These you shun as much as you can, or else you drag them along unwillingly, with mur-

murings, impatience and complaints. In you I seem to behold the kine that, despite themselves, drew the Ark along lowing as they went, not knowing that what they drew contained the most precious treasure on earth.[17]

179. Eternal Wisdom tells us that the number of fools and unfortunate people is infinite.[18] This is because the number of those who do not know the value of the Cross is infinite and they carry it despite themselves. But you, true disciple of Eternal Wisdom, if you have trials and afflictions, if you suffer many persecutions for justice' sake, if you are treated as the refuse of the world, be comforted, be glad, thrill with joy because the cross you carry is a gift so precious, it would arouse the envy of the Blessed, were they capable of envy. All that is honorable, glorious and virtuous in God and His Holy Spirit, rests upon you, for your reward is great in heaven. Even on earth your reward is great, because of the spiritual graces which the Cross obtains for you.

180. Friends of Jesus Christ, drink of His bitter cup, and your friendship with Him will increase. Suffer with Him and you will be glorified with Him. Suffer patiently and even cheerfully. Yet a little while and the moment of suffering will be changed into an eternity of happiness. Since it was necessary for Eternal Wisdom to enter heaven by the way of suffering, it is necessary for you to enter by the same

way. Whithersoever you turn, we read in the *Imitation of Christ*, you will always find the Cross. With the elect you will take it up rightly and carry it patiently and cheerfully for the love of God. With the damned you will carry it impatiently and against your will. You will become like so many twice confounded wretches who will be forced to say forever in hell: we have labored and suffered in the world. "We have walked through difficult paths." [19] And after all that, here we are with the damned.

True Wisdom is not to be found in the things of this world, nor "in the heart of them that live in delights." [20] He has fixed His abode in the Cross, so firmly that you will not find Him in this world save in the Cross. He has so truly incorporated and united Himself with the Cross that in all truth we can say: WISDOM IS THE CROSS, AND THE CROSS IS WISDOM.

---

[1] Tobias 12:7;   [2] Wisdom 8:1;   [3] 1 Cor. 1:23;
[4] Rom. 11:33;   [5] Wisdom 8:2;   [6] Ps. 39:9;
[7] Luke 22:15;   [8] Luke 12:50;   [9] Matt. 16:24;
[10] John 16:33;   [11] John 15:15;   [12] Luke 10:21;
[13] Office of Saint Andrew.   [14] Heb. 13:6;   [15] Eccles.
24:9;   [16] 2 Cor. 4:17;   [17] 1 Kings 6:12;   [18] Eccl.
1:15;   [19] Wisdom 5:7;   [20] Job 28:13.

Chapter Fifteen

The Means to Obtain Divine Wisdom

First Means: An Ardent Desire

181. Children of men, how long will your hearts remain heavy and inclined to earth? How long will you love vanity and seek after lying? Why do you not turn your eyes and your hearts upon Divine Wisdom Who of all that can be desired is the most desirable; Who, to obtain the love of man Himself teaches His origin, shows His beauty, displays His treasures and gives a thousand signs of His eagerness to be desired and sought after? "Covet ye therefore My words," [1] He teaches. "Wisdom preventeth them that covet her." [2] "The desire of wisdom bringeth to the everlasting kingdom." [3]

182. Desire of Divine Wisdom must indeed be a great grace of God, because it is the reward of the faithful keeping of the commandments of God. "Son, if you desire wisdom, keep justice, and God will give her to thee." [4] "Let thy thoughts be upon the precepts of God, and meditate continually upon His commandments and He will give thee a heart, and the desire of wisdom shall be given to thee." [5] "For wisdom will not enter into a malicious soul, nor dwell in a body subject to sins." [6]

This desire of Wisdom must be holy and sincere, fostered by the keeping of the commandments of God. An infinite number of fools and sluggards are animated with a thousand would-be desires for being good which, because they do not bring them to renounce sin or do violence to themselves, are but feigned and deceitful desires that kill and damn.[7] "The Holy Spirit Who is the master of discipline will flee from the deceitful, and will withdraw Himself from thoughts that are without understanding, and He shall not abide when iniquity cometh in."[8]

183. Solomon, the model given us by the Holy Spirit to obtain Wisdom, did not receive that gift until he had desired, sought after and prayed for it for a long time. "I wished, and understanding was given me, and I called upon God, and the Spirit of Wisdom came to me."[9] "I have loved and sought wisdom from my youth, and have desired to take her for my spouse. I went about seeking that I might take her to myself."[10] Like Solomon and Daniel we must be "men of desire"[11] to acquire this great treasure of Wisdom.

Second means: Persevering prayer

184. The greater a gift of God, the more effort it requires to obtain it. What prayers and efforts,

then, are required to obtain the gift of Wisdom which is the greatest of all God's gifts! Let us read the words of Divine Wisdom Himself: "Seek and you shall find, knock and it shall be opened to you; ask and it shall be given you." [12] As if He said: "If you wish to find Me, you must seek Me; if you wish to enter into My palace, you must knock at My door; if you wish to receive Me, you must ask for Me; nobody finds Me unless he seeks Me; nobody has access to Me unless he knocks at My door; nobody acquires Me unless he asks." Now all this is done by prayer. Prayer is the usual channel by which God conveys His gifts, more particularly His Wisdom. From the time of Adam, the world had asked for Divine Wisdom Incarnate. But it was only when Mary's womb was prepared by her prayers for His reception, that He came. Solomon received Wisdom only after praying for a long time and with extraordinary fervor. He tells us: "I went to the Lord and I besought Him, and said with my whole heart, give me Wisdom that sitteth by Thy throne." [13] "If any of you want Wisdom let him ask of God Who giveth to all men abundantly, and upbraideth not; and it shall be given him." [14] Note here that the Holy Spirit does not tell us to seek charity, humility, patience, or any other most excellent virtue, but to seek Wisdom. For, by asking for Divine Wisdom, we ask for all the virtues contained in Him.

Hence to acquire this Wisdom we must pray. But how should we pray?

185. First, we must pray for this gift *with a firm and lively faith*, "not wavering"; [15] because "he who wavers in his faith must not expect to receive." [16]

186. Second, we must pray for this gift *with a pure faith*, not relying, when we pray, on consolations, visions or special revelations, for, although such things may be good and true, as they were in some Saints, yet it is always dangerous to rely on them. Faith is less pure and meritorious the more it is based upon these extraordinary graces and feelings. In what the Holy Spirit tells us of the grandeur and the beauty of Wisdom, of God's desire to bestow upon us this great gift, of our own need of Him, we find strong enough motives to make us desire Him and ask God for Him with all faith and eagerness.

187. Pure faith is both the cause and the effect of Wisdom in our soul. The more faith we have the more we shall possess Divine Wisdom; and the more we possess Him, the more faith we shall have. "The just man—or the wise man—lives by faith"; [17] without seeing, without feeling, without tasting and without wavering. *God has said it or promised it.* In these words you have the foundation stone of all the prayers and actions of the wise man, although from the natural point of view it may seem to him that God has no eyes to see his miseries, no ears to

hear his prayers, no arms to crush his enemies, no hands to help him; although he may be assailed by distractions, by doubts, by darkness in his mind, by illusions in his imagination, by weariness and boredom in his heart, by sadness and agony in his soul. The wise man does not ask to see extraordinary sights such as those the Saints have seen, nor to experience sensible sweetness in his devotions, but he will ask with faith for Divine Wisdom, and he will be more assured that this Wisdom will be given than if an angel came down from heaven to vouch for it. He will remember God's word promising that all who pray to God as they should pray, will obtain what they ask for.[18] "If you then being evil, know how to give good things to your children, how much more will your father from heaven give the good spirit (of Wisdom) to them that ask Him?"[19]

188. Third, we *must pray perseveringly* to obtain this Wisdom. The acquisition of this precious pearl and infinite treasure, demands on our part a holy importunity with God; without which we shall not obtain it. We must not act as many people do when they ask God for a grace. If, when they have prayed for a considerable time, perhaps for years, God does not grant them what they ask for, they become discouraged and they cease to pray, thinking that God does not want to hear them. These souls lose the benefit of their prayers and they offend God Who loves to give and Who, in one way

or another, always answers prayers that are well said.

He, then, who wishes to obtain this Wisdom, must pray day and night without wearying, or becoming disheartened. Blessed a thousand times will he be, if he acquires Him, after ten, twenty, thirty years of prayer, or even just an hour before he dies. And if he does obtain this Treasure after having spent his whole life looking and asking for it, and making himself deserving of it by all sorts of labors and crosses, let him be convinced that it is not a gift due to him in justice, nor even a reward, but rather an alms given him out of pure mercy.

189. No, no, it is not those who are careless and inconstant with their prayers and seekings who will obtain this Wisdom, but rather those who are like the man who gets up during the night to knock at the door of his friend and asks to borrow three loaves of bread.[20] Note that it is Divine Wisdom Who, in this Gospel story, teaches us how to pray that we may receive. This man knocks again and again; he renews his knockings and entreaties four, five times with increasing noise and insistence, in spite of the untimely hour of the night and his friend having already gone to bed, and in spite of having been rebuffed and told repeatedly to be off, as an inconsiderate and troublesome person. At last the friend becomes so annoyed by the entreaties of the man that he gets out of bed, opens the door and gives him what he asks for.

MEANS: PERSEVERING PRAYER

190. If we pray thus to obtain this Wisdom, God, Who wishes to be importuned, will most certainly, sooner or later, rise up, open the door of His divine mercy and give us the three loaves of Wisdom; i.e. the bread of life, the bread of understanding and the bread of angels.

Here is a prayer composed by the Holy Spirit which teaches the soul how to ask for Divine Wisdom. It is the Prayer of Solomon asking for Wisdom.

191. *God of my fathers, and Lord of mercy, Who hast made all things with Thy word, and by Thy Wisdom hast appointed man that he should have dominion over the creature that was made by Thee, that he should order the world according to equity and justice, and execute justice with an upright heart; give me Wisdom that sitteth by Thy throne, and cast me not off from among Thy children; for I am Thy servant, and the son of Thy handmaid, a weak man and of short time, and falling short of the understanding of judgment and laws. For if one be perfect among the children of men, yet if Thy Wisdom is not with him, he shall be nothing regarded.*

192. *And Thy Wisdom with Thee, Which knoweth Thy works, Which then also was present when Thou madest the world, and knew what was agreeable to Thy eyes, and what was right in Thy commandments: send her out of Thy holy heaven, and*

from the throne of Thy Majesty, that she may be with me, and may labor with me, that I may know what is acceptable with Thee, for she knoweth and understandeth all things, and shall lead me soberly in my works, and shall preserve me by her power. So shall my work be acceptable, and I shall govern Thy people justly, and shall be worthy of the throne of my father. For who among men is he that can know the counsel of God? Or who can think what the will of God is? For the thoughts of mortal men are fearful and our counsels uncertain; for the corruptible body is a load upon the soul, and the earthly habitation presseth down the mind that museth upon many things. And hardly do we guess aright at things that are upon the earth, and with labor do we find the things that are before us. But the things that are in heaven, who shall search out? And who shall know Thy thoughts except Thou give Wisdom and send Thy Holy Spirit from above; and so the ways of them that are upon earth may be corrected, and men may learn the things that please Thee? For by Wisdom were they healed, whosoever have pleased Thee O Lord, from the beginning.[21]

193. To vocal prayer we must add mental prayer which enlightens the mind, inflames the heart and enables the soul to hear the voice of Wisdom, to relish His delights and to possess His treasures.

I know of no better means to establish in ourselves the kingdom of God and to draw Divine Wisdom to our soul than to pray vocally and mentally by saying the Holy Rosary, whilst meditating on its fifteen Mysteries.

[1] Wisdom 6:12;   [2] Wisdom 6:14;   [3] Wisdom 6:21;
[4] Eccl. 1:33;   [5] Eccl. 6:37;   [6] Wisdom 1:4;
[7] Prov. 21:25;   [8] Wisdom 1:5;   [9] Wisdom 7:7;
[10] Wisdom 8:2, 18;   [11] Dan. 9:23;   [12] Matt. 8:7,
Luke 11:9, Mark 11:24;   [13] Wisdom 8:21, 11:14;
[14] James 1:5;   [15] James 1:6;   [16] James 1:7;
[17] Rom. 1:7;   [18] Luke 11:10;   [19] Luke 11:13;
[20] Luke 11:5;   [21] Wisdom 9.

CHAPTER SIXTEEN

Third means to obtain Divine Wisdom: Universal Mortification

194. "Wisdom," the Holy Spirit declares, "is not found in the land of them that live in delights," [1] who gratify all the desires of their passions and bodily senses, for "they who are in the flesh cannot please God"; [2] and because, "the wisdom of the flesh is an enemy to God." [3] "My Spirit shall not remain in man, because he is flesh." [4] All those who belong to Christ, the Incarnate Wisdom, have crucified their flesh, with its vices and concupiscences. They ever bear about in their bodies the mortification of Jesus. They continually do violence to themselves, carry their cross every day, die daily, and bury themselves in Christ.[5] These words of the Holy Spirit show more clearly than the light of day that to possess Incarnate Wisdom, Jesus Christ, we must practice mortification, renounce the world and self.

195. Do not think that this Wisdom, purer than the rays of the sun, will enter a soul and a body sullied by the pleasures of the senses. Do not believe that He will grant His rest and ineffable peace to those who love the company and the vanities of the world. He tells us, "to him that overcometh"—the world and himself — "I will give the hidden Manna." [6] This lovable Prince, though He knows

and sees all things in a trice, by His infinite light, yet seeks for persons worthy of Him.[7] He seeks, because there are so few, that He can scarcely find any sufficiently detached from the world, sufficiently interior and mortified to be worthy of His Person, of His riches and of union with Him.

196. This Wisdom, to communicate Himself, is not satisfied with a half-hearted mortification, a mortification of a few days, but He requires universal, continuous, courageous and prudent mortification.

197. To obtain possession of Wisdom, it is necessary:

1. Either to give up entirely the possessions of the world as did the Apostles, the Disciples, the first Christians and Religious — and this is the best, quickest, and surest means to possess Wisdom—or, at the very least, to be detached in heart from all worldly goods. This detachment permits us to possess worldly goods as though not possessing them, without being eager to acquire, or being anxious to retain any; not complaining or worrying when possessions are lost. This is very difficult to accomplish.

198. 2. Not to follow the showy fashions of worldlings in dress, in furniture, in dwellings, in banquets or any other worldly modes and ways of living. "Be not conformed to this world."[8] This practice is more necessary than is generally thought.

199. 3. Not to believe or to follow the false maxims of the world; not to think, to speak, or to act as do the people of the world. Worldly doctrine is as opposed to that of the Incarnate Wisdom as darkness is opposed to light, and death to life. Consider well the opinions and the words of the worldlings. They think and speak evil of all the great truths of religion. True, they do not tell brazen lies. They cover their lying with a cloak of truth. They are not conscious of telling untruths, yet they lie. Nor do they usually teach sinful doctrines openly, but they speak of them as of virtue and propriety or else as of doctrines of indifference and of little consequence. This cunning which the devil has taught the world in order to cover up the heinousness of sin and lying, is the wickedness spoken of by St. John when he writes: "The whole world is seated in wickedness." [9] This is true now, more than ever.

200. 4. We must flee, as much as possible, from the company of men, not only from that of worldlings which is hurtful and dangerous, but even from that of devout persons when association with them is useless and a waste of time. He who wishes to become wise and perfect must put into practice these three golden counsels which Eternal Wisdom spoke to St. Arsenius: "Flee, hide, be silent." "Flee as much as possible from the company of men, as the greatest Saints have done." [10] Let your life be hid-

den with Christ in God; be silent in the company of men that you may converse with Divine Wisdom. "He who knows how to keep silent is a wise man." [12]

201. To obtain possession of this Wisdom we must mortify the body not only by enduring patiently our bodily ailments and the sufferings which the natural elements bring upon us, but also, by freely imposing upon ourselves some penances and mortifications. We may fast, watch before the Blessed Sacrament, talk with God during the silent hours of the night, and practice other austerities as exemplified in the lives of holy penitents. It requires courage to do this because the body naturally idolizes itself, and the world considers as useless all corporal penances and rejects them. The world does everything possible to deter people from practicing the austerities of the Saints. Of each one of the Saints it is said, in due proportion: "The wise, or the saintly man has brought his body into subjection by continual watchings, fastings, disciplines, cold, insufficient clothing and every kind of austerity. He made a compact with it not to give it any rest in this world." [13] The Holy Spirit declares of all the saints: "They hated the spotted garment which is carnal." [14]

202. In order that exterior and voluntary mortification be good, it is necessary that it be accompanied by mortification of the judgment and the will, and by holy obedience. Without this obedi-

ence, all exterior mortification is spoiled by self-love, and it often becomes more pleasing to the devil than to God. Hence, no considerable mortification should be undertaken without taking counsel. "I, Wisdom, dwell in counsel." [15] "He that trusteth in his own heart is a fool." [16] "The prudent man doth all things with counsel." [17] And the great counsel of the Holy Spirit is this: "My son, do thou nothing without counsel, and thou shalt not repent when thou hast done." [18] "Seek counsel always of a wise man." [19]

By this holy obedience we do away with self-love which spoils everything. By holy obedience the least of our actions become meritorious. It shields us from the illusions of the devil. It makes us conquer our enemies and brings us safely, as peacefully as if we were sleeping, into the harbor of salvation. All that I have just said is comprised in this one great counsel: *Leave all things and you will find all things, in finding Jesus Christ, the Incarnate Wisdom.*

[1] Job 28:13;   [2] Rom. 8:8;   [3] Rom. 8:7;   [4] Gen. 6:3;   [5] Luke 11:23, Rom. 6:4, 8, 2 Cor. 4:10, Gal. 5:24;   [6] Apoc. 2:17;   [7] Wisdom 6:17;   [8] Rom. 12:2;   [9] 1 John 5:19;   [10] Imitation Bk. 1, 20:1;   [11] Col. 3:3;   [12] Eccles. 20:5;   [13] Roman Breviary, St. Peter Alcantara Office.   [14] Jude 23;   [15] Prov. 8:12;   [16] Prov. 28:26;   [17] Prov. 13:16;   [18] Eccles. 32:24;   [19] Tob. 4:19.

CHAPTER SEVENTEEN

The fourth means to obtain Divine Wisdom: A tender and true devotion to the Blessed Virgin

203. The greatest means of all, and the most wonderful of all secrets for obtaining and keeping Divine Wisdom, is a tender and true devotion to the Blessed Mary.

No one but Mary has ever found grace with God for herself and for the whole human race. No one but Mary has had the power to conceive and give birth to Eternal Wisdom, and no one else has the power to bring Him to life, as it were, through the operation of the Holy Spirit in the souls of those chosen by Him.

The Patriarchs, Prophets and the just of the Old Law had prayed and sighed and begged for the Incarnation of Eternal Wisdom, but none of them had been able to merit it. No one was found but Mary who, by the loftiness of her virtues, reached the throne of the Divinity and merited to obtain this infinite gift. She became the Mother, the Mistress and the Throne of Divine Wisdom.

204. 1. Mary is His most worthy Mother because she conceived Him and brought Him forth as

the fruit of her womb; "Blessed is the fruit of thy womb, Jesus." Hence, it is true to say that Jesus is the fruit and the product of Mary wherever He is found—in heaven, on earth, in our tabernacles and in our hearts—and that Mary alone is the tree of life, and Jesus alone the fruit of that tree. Therefore, he who wishes to have in his heart that admirable fruit, must first have the tree that produces it. Whoever wishes to have Jesus must have Mary.

205. 2. Mary is the Mistress of Divine Wisdom; not that she is higher than the Divine Wisdom Who is true God, nor even His equal—it would be blasphemous to think or say so—but because the Son of God, Eternal Wisdom, by making Himself perfectly subject to Mary as to His Mother, gave her a maternal and natural power over Him, which passes our understanding. He gave her this power, not only for the length of His life on earth, but also in heaven, because heavenly glory far from destroying nature, perfects it. Hence, in heaven, Jesus is as much the Son of Mary as Mary is the Mother of Jesus. In this relationship, then, Mary has authority over Jesus Who, in a sense, remains subject to her, because He wills it. This means that Mary, by her powerful prayers, and because of her being His Immaculate Mother, obtains from Jesus all that she wills. It means that she gives Him to whom she wills, and that she produces Him, every day, in the souls of those she wills.

206. O, happy the souls who have won the favor of Mary! They can rest assured that soon they will possess Divine Wisdom, for, as she loves those who love her, she communicates to them lavishly her possessions, and the infinite Treasure in Whom all others are contained, Jesus, the fruit of her womb.

207. If, then, it is true to say that Mary is, in a sense, the Mistress of the Incarnate Wisdom, what then is to be thought of her power over all the graces and gifts of God, and of the freedom she enjoys to give them to whom she pleases? The Fathers of the Church tell us that Mary is the immense ocean of the perfections of God, the great storehouse of all His possessions, the inexhaustible treasury of the Lord, the treasurer and the dispenser of all His gifts. It is the will of God that since He gave His Son to Mary, we should receive all through her hands, and that no heavenly gift should flow down upon the earth without passing through Mary as through a channel. Of her plenitude we have all received. If there is any grace, any hope of salvation in us, it is a gift which comes to us through Mary. She is so truly the Mistress of God's possessions, that she gives to whom she wills and as she wills, all the graces of God, all the virtues of Jesus Christ, all the gifts of the Holy Spirit, all good things in the order of nature, of grace and of glory.

These are the thoughts and the expressions of the Fathers of the Church. It is evident, then, that whatever gift this sovereign and lovable Princess bestows upon us, she is not satisfied until she has given to us the Incarnate Wisdom, Jesus, her Son; and she is ever busy looking for souls worthy of that Wisdom in order to give Him to them.

208. 3. Mary, moreover, is the royal throne of Eternal Wisdom. In her He exhibits His perfections and displays His treasures. In her He takes His delight. There is no place in heaven or on earth where Eternal Wisdom shows so much magnificence, and takes such delight as in the incomparable Mary. This is the reason why the Fathers of the Church call her the Tabernacle of the Divinity, the Resting Place and the Joy of the Blessed Trinity, the Throne of God, the City of God, the Altar of God, the Temple of God, the World of God, and the Paradise of God. All these laudatory appellations are most true, when applied to the different marvels which the most High has worked in Mary.

209. THROUGH MARY ALONE THEN, CAN WE OBTAIN POSSESSION OF WISDOM. But, if we do receive such a gift as this Wisdom, where are we to lodge Him? What dwelling, what seat, what throne are we to offer to this Prince Who is so pure and resplendent that the very rays of the sun are but as dust and darkness in His presence? Perhaps I may be told that as He asks only for our heart, it is our heart we must offer Him, and we must lodge Him therein.

210. But do we not know that our heart is sullied, impure, carnal and full of evil inclinations, and consequently unworthy of harboring such a noble and holy Guest; that if we had a hundred thousand hearts like ours to offer Him as so many thrones, yet He would rightly reject our advances, turn a deaf ear to our entreaties and even accuse us of being foolhardy and impudent, by wishing to lodge Him in a place so foul and so unworthy of His Majesty?

211. What then are we to do to make our hearts worthy of Him? Here is the great advice, the admirable secret. Let us, so to speak, take Mary into our house by consecrating ourselves unreservedly to her as her servants and slaves. Let us surrender into her hands, and in her honor, all we possess, even that which is dearest to us. Let us not keep anything for ourselves, and this good Mistress who never allows herself to be outdone in liberality, will give herself to us, in an incomprehensible yet real manner, and then Eternal Wisdom will come to dwell in her as in His glorious throne room.

212. 4. Mary is the secret magnet [2] which, wherever it is, draws Eternal Wisdom so powerfully that He cannot resist. This magnet drew Him down upon earth for the benefit of all men in general, and it still draws Him in particular every day to every man who possesses it. Once we possess Mary we shall easily and in a short time possess Divine Wisdom through her intercession. Of all the means

to possess Jesus Christ, Mary is the surest, the easiest, the shortest way and the holiest. Were we to practice the most frightful penances; were we to undertake the most painful journeys and the most laborious works; were we to shed all our blood for the acquisition of Divine Wisdom, all these efforts would be useless and insufficient to obtain Him without Mary's intercession and solicitude. But if Mary speaks a word in our favor, if we love her, if we bear the mark of her faithful servants who do her will, we shall quickly and easily possess Divine Wisdom.

213. 5. Note that Mary in addition to being the Mother of Jesus, the Head of all the elect, is also the Mother of all His members. She begets them, bears them in her womb and brings them forth to the glory of heaven by the graces of God which she imparts to them. This is the teaching of the Fathers of the Church, particularly of St. Augustine who says that the elect are in the womb of Mary until she brings them forth when they enter into their heavenly glory.[3] Moreover, God has decreed that Mary should dwell in Jacob, take her inheritance in Israel and place the root of her virtues in the elect.

214. From these truths we must infer: (1) That in vain we flatter ourselves with being the children of God and the disciples of Divine Wisdom if we are not the children of Mary. (2) That to be of the number of the elect it is necessary that by a tender

and sincere devotion to the Blessed Virgin we should bring her to dwell in us and to place the roots of her virtues in our soul. (3) That Mary must beget us in Jesus Christ, and Jesus Christ in us, unto the perfection and the fullness of His age. Then Mary may say of herself more truthfully than St. Paul said of himself: "My little children, I beget you every day till Jesus Christ," my Son, "be perfectly formed in you." [5]

215. Someone perhaps, anxious to be devoted to our Lady, may ask me: "In what does true devotion to the Blessed Virgin consist?"

I answer briefly: "It consists in highly appreciating her excellence; in showing deep gratitude for her favors; in being zealous to promote her glory; in having continual recourse to her intercession; in being totally dependent upon her authority; in showing a firm reliance and a tender confidence in her maternal goodness."

216. We must beware of those false devotions to the Blessed Virgin of which the devil makes use to deceive and to damn many souls. I shall not describe them here, but shall only say that true devotion to Mary is: (1) Always *interior*, free from hypocrisy and superstition. (2) *Tender*, not lukewarm or scrupulous. (3) *Constant*, not fickle and disloyal. (4) *Holy*, without presumption and without sinfulness.

217. We must not be among those false and hypo-

critical devotees who give only lip-service or have only exterior devotion.

Neither must we be among the number of the critical and scrupulous devotees who fear to give too much honor to our Lady, and to dishonor the Son by honoring the Mother.

We must not be indifferent and self-interested devotees, who have no tender love or filial confidence in our Lady, and who have recourse to her only to acquire or retain temporal goods.

We must not be like the inconstant and fickle devotees who are devout to the Blessed Virgin by fits and starts, and who, after serving her for a short while, fall away at the time of temptation.

Lastly, we must beware of being among the number of those presumptuous devotees who, under the cloak of some exterior practices of devotion to Mary, conceal a heart corrupted by sin; and who fancy that, because of their presumed devotion to Mary, they will not die without confession but will be saved no matter what sins they commit.

218. We must not neglect to become members of our Lady's confraternities, and especially of the Confraternity of the Holy Rosary, and faithfully to abide by its rules which are very sanctifying.

219. BUT THE MOST PERFECT AND THE MOST ADVANTAGEOUS OF ALL DEVOTIONS TO THE BLESSED VIRGIN CONSISTS IN CONSECRATING OURSELVES ENTIRELY TO HER AND TO JESUS THROUGH HER, AS

DEVOTION TO BLESSED VIRGIN

THEIR SLAVES; DEDICATING TO HER COMPLETELY
AND FOR ALL ETERNITY, OUR BODY AND SOUL, OUR
GOODS, BOTH INTERIOR AND EXTERIOR, THE SATIS-
FACTIONS AND THE MERITS OF OUR GOOD WORKS
AND OUR RIGHT TO DISPOSE OF THEM. IN SHORT,
DEDICATION OF ALL THE POSSESSIONS WE HAVE
ACQUIRED IN THE PAST, THOSE WE ACTUALLY POS-
SESS AND THOSE WHICH WE MAY ACQUIRE IN THE
FUTURE.

As there are several books treating of this devotion,
I shall only state that I have never found a practice
of devotion more solid than this one, because it is
based upon the example of Jesus Christ and it gives
more glory to God, is more beneficial to the soul and
is more terrible than any other to the enemies of our
salvation. Nor have I found an easier or more attractive one.

220. This devotion, if well practiced, will not
only draw Jesus Christ, Eternal Wisdom, into our
soul, but will also maintain and keep Him in us
until death. For what, I ask you, would it benefit
us to go after many secrets and to spend ourselves
in many labors to obtain Divine Wisdom, if, after
acquiring Him, we were like Solomon so unfortunate as to lose Him again by our infidelity? Solomon
was wiser than we shall ever be, consequently, he
was stronger and more enlightened, and yet he was
deceived, he was conquered, he fell into sin and
folly, and he left to all those who came after him

the paradox of his light and of his darkness, of his wisdom and of the folly of his sins. It may be said that his example and writing urged his descendants to desire and to seek for wisdom, but the fact of his fall, grounded as it is in truth, has kept a great number of souls from diligently pursuing that which is indeed precious, but which is also very easily lost.

221. To be then, in a way, wiser than Solomon we should place in Mary's hands all our possessions and the Treasure of all treasures, Jesus Christ, that she may keep Him for us. We are vessels too fragile to contain this precious Treasure and this heavenly Manna. We are surrounded by too many shrewd and experienced enemies, to trust in our own prudence and strength. We have had too many sad experiences of our own inconstancy and natural thoughtlessness, not to be distrustful of our own wisdom and fervor.

222. Mary is *wise*. Let us place all in her hands. She knows how to dispose of us and all that is ours to the greater glory of God.

Mary is *charitable*. She loves us as her children and servants. Let us give her all, and we shall lose nothing. She will turn everything to our gain.

Mary is *liberal*. She gives back more than is given to her. Let us give her unreservedly all that we possess. She will render us a hundredfold.

Mary is *powerful*. No one can take away from her what we place in her hands. Let us, then, com-

DEVOTION TO BLESSED VIRGIN

mit ourselves to her care and she will defend us against all our enemies and help us to conquer them.

Mary is *faithful*. She does not allow anything that we give her to be lost or wasted. She is *par excellence* the Virgin faithful to God and faithful to man. She faithfully guarded and kept all that God entrusted to her, never allowing a particle of it to be lost. She still keeps every day, with special care, all those who place themselves entirely under her protection and guidance.

Let us, then, confide everything to this faithful Virgin. Let us attach ourselves to her as to an immovable pillar, as to an anchor that cannot be lifted, or rather as to Mount Sion which cannot be shaken.

Thus, whatever may be our natural blindness, our weakness and inconstancy; whatever may be the number and the wickedness of our enemies, we shall never be deceived nor misled, and we shall never have the misfortune of losing the grace of God and the infinite Treasure of Eternal Wisdom.

[1] St. Peter Damien Serm. 142 X, St. Ambrose Comment. in Luce.　[2] Blessed Proclus of Constantinople, Hom. de Christi Nat.　[3] Saint Augustine, Tract. de Symbolo ad Catechumenos;　[4] Eccles. 24:13;　[5] Gal. 4:19.

LOVE OF ETERNAL WISDOM

Act of Consecration to Jesus Christ, the Incarnate Wisdom, by the Hands of Mary

223. O Eternal and Incarnate Wisdom! O sweetest and most adorable Jesus! True God and True Man, only Son of the Eternal Father and of Mary always Virgin! I adore Thee profoundly in the bosom and splendors of Thy Father during eternity, and in the virginal womb of Mary Thy most worthy Mother, in the time of Thy Incarnation.

I give Thee thanks that Thou has emptied Thyself in taking the form of a slave in order to save me from the cruel slavery of the devil. I praise and glorify Thee that Thou hast been pleased to submit Thyself to Mary, Thy Holy Mother, in all things, in order to make me Thy faithful slave through her. But, alas! ungrateful and unfaithful as I have been, I have not kept the promises which I made so solemnly to Thee in my Baptism. I have not fulfilled my obligations; I do not deserve to be called Thy child nor even Thy slave; and as there is nothing in me which does not merit Thine anger and repulse, I dare no longer come by myself before Thy most holy and august Majesty. This is why I have recourse to the intercession of Thy Most Holy Mother, whom Thou has given me to mediate with Thee. It is through her that I hope to obtain of Thee contrition and the pardon of my sins, the acquisition and the preservation of Wisdom.

DEVOTION TO BLESSED VIRGIN

Hail then, Immaculate Mary, living Tabernacle of the Divinity, in which the Eternal Wisdom deigned to be hidden and to be adored by Angels and by men! Hail, Queen of Heaven and earth to whose empire is subject everything that is under God! Hail, sure Refuge of sinners; whose mercy fails no one! Grant the desire which I have to obtain Divine Wisdom, and for this end deign to accept the offering and promises which my lowliness presents to Thee.

I (N.N.) an unfaithful sinner, renew and ratify today in thy hands the promises of my Baptism: I renounce for ever Satan, his pomps and his works; and I give myself entirely to Jesus Christ, the Incarnate Wisdom, to carry my cross after Him all the days of my life and to be more faithful to Him than I have been till now.

I choose thee, this day, O Mary, in the presence of all the heavenly court, for my Mother and Mistress. I deliver and consecrate to thee, as thy slave, my body and soul, my goods, both interior and exterior, and even the value of my good actions, past, present and future. I leave to thee the entire and full right to dispose of me and all that belongs to me, without exception, as thou pleasest, for the greater glory of God, in time and in eternity.

Receive, O gracious Virgin, this little offering of my slavery in honor of and in union with that subjection which the Eternal Wisdom deigned to have to thy maternity, in homage to the power which both of you have over this little worm and miserable sinner, and in thanksgiving for the privileges with which the Holy Trinity has favored thee. I protest that henceforth I wish, as thy true slave, to seek thy honor and to obey thee in all things.

O admirable Mother, present me to thy dear Son as His eternal slave, so that as He has redeemed me by thee, by thee He may receive me! O Mother of Mercy, grant that I may obtain the true Wisdom of God, and for this end receive me among those whom thou lovest and teachest, whom thou leadest, nourishest and protectest as thy children and thy slaves.

O faithful Virgin, make me in all things so perfect a disciple, imitator and slave of the Incarnate Wisdom, Jesus Christ thy Son, that I may attain by thine intercession and example to the fullness of His age on earth and of His glory in heaven Amen.

"He that can take it let him take it." [1]
"Who is wise and will understand this?" [2]

[1] Matt. 19:12;   [2] Ps. 106:43.

SPIRITUAL MAXIMS

of

ETERNAL WISDOM

according to St. Louis De Montfort

The following maxims or spiritual counsels were originally composed by St. Louis De Montfort and intended for his newly-founded community, the Daughters of Wisdom. For the benefit of the general public we have decided to insert them in this edition, adapting them to the conditions of those living in the world and seeking to acquire a closer union with Christ, the Eternal and Incarnate Wisdom.

The Editors

FIRST MAXIM

Voice of the Eternal Wisdom

True happiness on earth lies in voluntary poverty and in following Me.

1. My son, have no attachment to any created good, however holy it may be, whether interior or exterior, spiritual or corporal.

2. Always be on your guard against anything which draws your affection.

3. Beware of the purely natural affections of your relatives and friends when they are an obstacle to your salvation or to your perfection.

4. Do not be afraid to disoblige or to displease others if you must do so to carry your cross after Me.

5. After My example, carry your cross of contradiction, persecution, renunciation and contempt, every day.

6. Do not be ashamed to practice any act of virtue before others, and do not omit any good deed for fear of scorn or praise, when you know that God demands it of you.

SECOND MAXIM

Voice of the Eternal Wisdom

You are truly blessed if the world persecutes you, opposing your plans though they are good, thinking evil of your intentions, calumniating your conduct, and taking away unjustly your reputation or your possessions.

1. My son, beware of complaining to others than to Me of the bad treatment you receive, and do not seek ways of justifying yourself, particularly when you are the only one to suffer from it.

2. On the contrary, pray for those who procure for you the blessings of persecution.

3. Thank Me for treating you as I myself was treated on earth, a sign of contradiction.

4. Never be discouraged in your plans because you meet with opposition; it is a pledge of future victory. A good work which is not opposed, which is not marked by the sign of the cross, has no great value before Me and will soon be destroyed.

5. Regard as your best friends those who persecute you because they procure for you great merit on earth, and great glory in heaven.

6. Regard as unfortunate those who live in luxury, who feast sumptuously, who frequent the world of fashion, who make their way in the world, who succeed in business, and who spend their lives in pleasures and amusements.

7. Never do anything, either good or evil, out of human respect to avoid any blame, insult, mockery, or praise.

8. When through your own fault some loss or disgrace befalls you, do not be disturbed by it, but rather humble yourself before God and accept it from His hands as punishment for your fault.

Third Maxim

Voice of the Eternal Wisdom

If anyone comes to me and does not hate his father and mother, and wife and children, and brothers and sisters, yes, and even his own life, he cannot be my disciple. (Luke 14:26).

1. My son, hate your own mind with its thoughts, rejecting them if they are bad, dangerous, or useless.

2. Do not rely exclusively on your own ideas, thoughts, knowledge, visions, or contemplations, and never constitute yourself the final judge of their goodness or their malice.

3. Believe that the judgment of others, in any indifferent matter, is always more accurate and more solid than your own, however much you would like to believe the contrary.

4. Beware of your imagination and your memory, rejecting evil thoughts, extravagant and useless plans, and vain, dangerous, or at least idle representations of the past or the future.

5. Strive to empty your memory of every object other than the presence of God.

6. Do not voluntarily dwell on the evil that has been done to you or on the good that you have done.

7. Despise your own will, submitting it to that of

your superiors and always renouncing it, even in matters that seem excellent to you.

8. Do nothing of any importance without taking counsel so that you may not have to repent of it after it is done.

9. Do not anxiously crave for things you do not possess, even though they might seem useful to your neighbor and glorious to My majesty.

10. Ask Me earnestly for particular favors, but request them only because it is My will that you should ask for them, and let conformity to My will be the basis of your prayer.

Fourth Maxim

Voice of the Eternal Wisdom

Take up your cross daily and follow Me.

1. My son, renounce the pleasures of your senses, innocent though they be.

2. Mortify your eyes by avoiding the sight of dangerous or curious things.

3. Mortify your ears, closing them to evil, vain, and useless discourse.

4. Mortify your tongue, by avoiding idle conversations, speaking frequently of Me or of things that concern Me, and maintaining a continual silence, if

you can, on the good that you have done, on the faults of your neighbors, and on your own good qualities.

5. Mortify your taste, by not eating unnecessarily between meals, by fasting in a spirit of obedience, by eating something unpleasant, by eating with restraint and modesty when appetite and hunger make you eager for food.

6. Mortify your sense of smell, by abstaining from superfluous use of perfumes.

7. Mortify your hands by avoiding superfluous and unseemly gestures.

8. Mortify your feet, avoiding hurried and unbecoming steps. Do not walk with affectation or haste, but with simplicity and modesty.

9. Mortify your sense of touch by preferring less expensive clothing and furniture and by performing acts of penance daily.

10. Mortify your whole body, by doing your work in a spirit of penance, and by accepting joyfully the discomforts of the seasons, and the various illnesses that attack the body.

FIFTH MAXIM

Voice of the Eternal Wisdom

The way and the gate that lead to heaven are narrow, and few there are who find the way and enter by the gate.

1. My son, do continual violence to your natural inclinations and dispositions, that you may be one of the small number who find the way of life, and who enter by the narrow gate to heaven.

2. Take care not to follow the majority and the common herd, so many of whom are lost.

3. Do not be deceived—there are only two ways: one that leads to life, and is narrow; the other that leads to death, and is wide; there is no middle way.

4. If your eye or your hand or your foot scandalize you, cut it off without delay lest you perish. In other words: avoid the occasions of sin.

SIXTH MAXIM

Voice of the Eternal Wisdom

Watch and pray without ceasing.

1. My son, you must apply yourself continually to vocal or mental prayer.

2. Do everything in the spirit of prayer, that is

to say, for the love of God and in the presence of God.

3. Never give up prayer, no matter what difficulty or what dryness you may experience.

4. Never give yourself up entirely to external things, for the kingdom of God is within you.

5. Esteem more highly than all exterior things those that are within the heart.

6. Believe that the greatest things that are done on this earth are wrought interiorly, and in the hearts of faithful souls.

7. Do everything in a spirit of faith, and let this virtue be the food of your meditations, and the quality that gives value to your actions.

SEVENTH MAXIM

Voice of the Eternal Wisdom

Love your enemies, do good to them
that do evil to you.

1. My son, pray for them that persecute you, heap insults upon you, and rob you of your honor and property.

2. Never do to others what you would not have them do to you.

3. Bear with the faults of others for the love of God Who is patient with you.

4. Rebuke those who offend Me, without fearing their reprisals.

EIGHTH MAXIM

Voice of the Eternal Wisdom

I converse familiarly with the simple, and I reveal My secrets only to the little ones.

1. My son, be simple as a dove, without malice, without duplicity, without dissimulation.

2. The greater you are the more you should humble yourself, that is to say, be the servant of others. Choose the lowest place, the lowliest employment, the poorest clothing.

3. As God gives His grace to the humble, do all your actions with deep humility of heart, in order to obtain My grace, and My friendship.

4. Beware of what is great, illustrious and dazzling in the eyes of men, for that is valueless in My sight.

5. Love the life that is hidden, poor, and worthless in the eyes of the world for such is the object of My delight.

6. You must become like a little child, if you would enter heaven, that is to say, simple, obedient, innocent, and gentle as a little child.

7. Those who for the kingdom of God have made themselves the last and the servants of others are the first and the most exalted in My sight.

8. If you exalt yourself higher than I desire, you will be brought lower than you desire, in this world

and in the next; if, on the contrary, you set yourself below others, I will exalt you above others, even in this world.

NINTH MAXIM

Voice of the Eternal Wisdom

He who is faithful in little things will be faithful also in those that are great, and he who is unfaithful in little things will be unfaithful also in those that are great.

1. My son, be very faithful to the little rules, the little inspirations, the little practices of virtue.

2. Do not neglect anything that can help you to acquire perfection.

3. If you are faithful in a few things, I assure you that I will set you over many things; that is to say, that if I see you corresponding faithfully to the few graces you receive, to the little amount of devotion you feel, etc., I will give you a share in a greater abundance of graces.

4. Take care not to neglect the little things, for otherwise you will gradually fall into lukewarmness and a lack of devotion; you will lose, little by little, your inspirations, your devotion, your merits, and your graces.

SPIRITUAL MAXIMS

Tenth Maxim

Voice of the Eternal Wisdom

I choose the least things of this world to confound and destroy what is greatest.

1. My son, humble yourself and remain humble, and I will make something of you.

2. Give your garment to him who takes from you your cloak.

3. Turn the other cheek to him who strikes you.

4. Suffer everything without complaining.

5. Be the first to accuse yourself, and to take the blame upon yourself.

6. Believe all that is good of others and all that is evil of yourself.

7. Choose, if you have the grace to do so, the least agreeable in everything.

8. Rejoice amid all sorts of difficulties and contradictions especially when you are found worthy to suffer something for My sake.

9. Never despair, and never be disturbed, when you fall into sin, but humble yourself, begging My forgiveness.

Eleventh Maxim

Voice of the Eternal Wisdom

Beware of false prophets.

My son, you must deeply distrust:

1. The lights of your own mind, however spiritually-minded you may be;

2. The feelings of your heart, however just and sincere they may seem to you;

3. The spiritual maxims of the lukewarm;

4. The beautiful and lofty thoughts and the holy undertakings which the evil spirit, disguised as an angel of light, often inspires in the most zealous and spiritual souls to bring about their downfall by his wiles and deceits.

Twelfth Maxim

Counsels of Saint Louis De Montfort

To distinguish and avoid the subtle snares of self-love, of the flesh, and of the devil, these are the important counsels I give you.

1. Never willingly take pleasure in, or still less rely on, what you have thought, imagined, or decided; but put your pleasure, your confidence, and your reliance only in the merits and intercession of

Mary, whose slave you are, with Jesus; in the blood and the merits of Jesus before the Father; and in the infinite mercy of God your Father.

2. Do not set yourself up as your own judge, for no one is a legitimate judge of his own case; but reveal all your thoughts, ideas, etc., to your spiritual director or to your confessor; do not hide from him anything you have in your heart or anything that has affected you.

3. Obey your confessor in all spiritual matters and profit by his advice.